Philosophy of Science

A. Appan Ramanujam

SHARADA

SHARADA PUBLISHING HOUSE

DELHI

First Published 2024

ISBN: 978-93-83221-54-7
₹ 1500

Published by
SHARADA PUBLISHING HOUSE
111, Vidya Vihar Apartment
Sector-9, Rohini, Delhi-110 085 (INDIA)
Ph.: +91-11-4702 6210 (O), +91-9899028954 (M)
E-mail : bansal_sph@rediffmail.com
books@sharadabooks.com
Website : www.sharadabooks.com

Printed at
Delhi

CONTENTS

PREFACE

'Philosophy of Science' as a subject of study requires the knowledge of the fundamental concepts of philosophy and the facts of various branches of science. Many colleges and universities do not offer Philosophy of Science as a subject of study because of the need for expertise in both science and philosophy.

This book analyses various steps in arriving at the conclusions of science such as Laws, Principles, Hypothesis and Theories. Observation, analysis of data, Hypothesis and Laws of Science are the various steps. Induction and Deduction play an important role in scientific explanation. The limitations of Induction are elaborated by Francis Bacon and David Hume. Karl Popper says that all scientific theories are only provisionally true because any scientific theory can be *falsified* by any later developments in Science. For Thomas Kuhn, Scientific Theories are *Paradigm shifts* in course of time.

It is man's nature to enquire about the world around us. Therefore, the Greek Philosopher Thale's question "Out of which the world is made of?" is quite relevant. However, Thale's answer that the universe is made of water is meaningless. But his question laid the foundation for modern chemistry. What are mathematical objects? Are they empirical or mere concepts? These questions are answered in a chapter on the Structure of Mathematic. About the structure of the universe, various theories of universe are discussed such as Big Bang Theory and steady state Cosmological Theory. Indian theories of universe are briefly discussed.

In a chapter on Scientific Explanation, the differences between explanations of physico-chemical events and social events are analysed in detail because the physical sciences are *nomothetic* and social sciences are *ideographic* in nature. In short, nomothetic sciences deal with events which are *repeatable* whereas social events are *irrepeatable.*

I hope this book will be useful to the readers who are interested in Philosophy of Science.

Acknowledgements

I must record my sense of gratitude to Dr. Pete A.Y. Gunter, Chairman, Department of Philosophy, North Texas State University, Texas, U.S.A. Even when I was a Ph.D. scholar, he used to send the re-prints of his published papers for study. My communication with him enriched my thoughts on the concepts of philosophy including Philosophy of Science.

Next, I must acknowledge the encouragement and support I received from Dr. T.N. Ganapathy (Late), H.O.D. of Philosophy, R.K.M. Vivekananda College, Mylapore, Chennai for asking me to teach the subject on Philosophy of Science to P.G. students. The two decades of my teaching the subject helped me to write this book. I must be grateful to the authorities of Anna Centenary Library, Chennai for permitting me to utilise the facilities available in the library.

I must acknowledge the emotional support and encouragement I received from my wife Mrs. Padmaleela and daughters A.R. Shloka and A.R. Prajna.

I thank Mr. D. Jegannath, Mrs. Sangeetha and Mr. Manivel, Administrative Staff, Sri Ramachandra University (Deemed to be University), Porur, Chennai. for typing the manuscripts.

I am grateful to the Sharada Publishing House for accepting my manuscript for publications. I must thank the Sharada Publishing House for the neat execution of the work. The Sharada Publishing House has already published three of my books. They are 1) Reflections on Bergson's Philosophy, 2) Perspectives of Indian and Western Philosophical Thought and 3) Philosophy and Cultural Traditions of East Asia (Won the Best Book Award at 95th session of the Indian Philosophical Congress held at Wardha, December 2022).

Part I

Chapter I

Introduction

This book on Philosophy of Science fulfils the U.G.C. requirements for the study of Philosophy of Science as a subject for P.G. course in Indian Universities in Part I. The objective of the study is to make the students aware of the similarities between philosophy and science and the values of science and technology. It makes the students aware of the different theories of confirmation and probabilities. The students are introduced to the problems of induction, probability and realism in Philosophy of Science.

Part I of this book has five chapters. The first chapter examines the relation between science, philosophy and philosophy of science. The impact of science on western civilisation is discussed briefly. In the second chapter the role of induction in Science is analysed. What is Presuppositionless observation? The contributions made by Bacon, Hume, and

Goodman for induction and confirmation are elaborated in detail. In inductive generalization, we observe some cases and then jump to a generalisation which leads to Hypothesis, Law and Theory in Science.

In the Chapter III the interrelations between Logic, Realism and Empiricism are probed. An attempt is also made to examine the relation between Logical Positivism and Logical Empiricism in Science.

In the Chapter IV the role of rationality in science and Karl Popper's theory of falsification are discussed. Unlike induction in science, in deduction inference plays a vital role. Science and Non-science should be demarcated in order to understand Popperian theory of falsification.

In the Chapter V Thomas Kuhn's view on Philosophy of science as narrated in his *The Structure of Scientific Revolution* is briefly given. Unlike Popper, scientific progress lies not in falsification of theories, but in a series of paradigm shifts in the findings of the scientists. Relativism in science as well as the rivalry among the paradigms are discussed.

Philosophizing requires data in science. Science is an empirical study. Without empirical data relating to various branches of science such as mathematics, physics, biology and cosmology philosophizing science will be just a 'talk' on science. Therefore Chapter VI and VII deal with various theories in mathematics and physics. What are mathematical objects? What are Numbers? What is a straight line? Are numbers only ideas? or are they real entities? These questions have been discussed in Chapter VI from the perspectives of 1) Platonism, 2) Intuitionism 3) Formalism and 4) Nominalism and 5) Logic.

Chapter VII deals with the problem of the structure of the universe. What are the constituents of the universe? Out of which the universe is made of? Thales, the Greek Philosopher answered that the universe is made of *water*. Later on in modern times the subject developed into chemistry. Various, elements were discovered. Dalton's atomic theory, atoms, molecules and various theories in physics and mathematics contributed in understanding the structure of the universe.

Chapter VIII enumerates the various types of Scientific Explanation. What is Explanation in Science? There are four types of Explanation in Science: 1) Deductive 2) Probabilistic 3) Teleological and 4) Genetic. What is the difference between mechanistic and teleological interpretations of scientific explanation? What is Ideographic Science? And what are the methodological problems of explanation in social science? These questions are answered briefly in Chapter VIII

In the Chapter IX the relation between Science and Humanity is examined. For a holistic life man's moral, religious and artistic aspects of life are necessary. Man's relationship with the environment and his harmonious existence with man, animal and nature will lead to peaceful existence. Art and religion play a vital role for man's holistic life.

The Chapters VI and VII include the Indian theories of Mathematics and Universe. The decimal number system and the concept of Zero were first introduced by the Indian mathematicians. The Kerala School of mathematics introduced *calculus* even before Leibniz and Newton. The Vedic people, the Jains and the ancient Tamils contributed to the development of mathematics.

In the chapter VII the Indian theory of atomism is briefly discussed. The Vaisheshika theory of *paramanu* as given by Kanada reveals the ancient Indians knowledge of atomic theory. The Indians believed in cyclic theory of universe which is related to time. The cyclic view anticipates Big Bang theories future and past Big Bang events. For Hindus the universe was created by Brahma, the creator who himself grew from a lotus flower from Lord Vishnu's navel. Brahma separated the flower into three parts-the heavens, the earth and the sky.

Vedanta relates the universe with the soul and considers the power of Atman to be greater than that of the solar system. Since man is part of the solar system, the *Phalita-jyotisha* believes in the influence of planets on practical life. But the Jains believe that the universe was not created by God. It is regulated by cosmic laws and kept going by its own energy processes. This concept of the universe is compatible with scientific thinking.

Chapter II

Introduction to Philosophy of Science

Philosophy

Philosophy is derived from Greek word *Philosophia* which means 'love of wisdom'. It is the study of general and fundamental questions such as those about reason, existence, knowledge, values, mind and language. Such questions are often posed as problems to be studied or resolved. Philosophical methods include questioning, critical discussion, rational argument, and systematic presentation. The branches of philosophy include *metaphysics,* which is concerned with the fundamental nature of *existence* and *reality, epistemology* which studies the nature of *knowledge* and *beliefs, ethics,* which is concerned with *moral value;* and logic which studies the rules of inference that allow one to deduce *conclusions* from the premises. Other notable subfields include philosophy of science, political philosophy, aesthetics, philosophy of language and philosophy of mind.

Epistemology

Epistemology asks how do we know? What are the sources of knowledge? It studies the nature, origin, scope and possibility of knowledge.

Metaphysics

It is the study of "first principles", and "being" (ontology). In other words it is the study of the most general aspects of reality pertaining to subjects such as substance, identity, the nature of the mind and free will. It is the study of nature and the nature of the world in which humans live.

Philosophy of Science

Philosophy of science is a study of science concerned with whether scientific knowledge can be said to be certain, how we obtain it, can science really explain everything, does causation really exist, can every event in the universe be described in terms of physics and chemistry. Philosophy of science questions the aims of science, discovery, validity and certainty of a theory in science. It relates science with philosophy. History of science without philosophy of science is blind, and philosophy of science without history of science is empty.

Nature of Science

Sciences are the result of the inborn human tendency to ask questions, to enquire and explore. The aim of science is to obtain knowledge about empirical phenomena. Knowledge can be called scientific if it is systematic, well integrated and comprehensive. By science we mean not only the true and systematic knowledge gained so far but also the discontent with what is known. It is an attempt to improve the quantity and quality of what is known. So we can frame a sort of provisional definition of science as a systematic knowledge of empirical reality obtained through the scientific method consisting of observation, hypothesis-formation, generalisation and verification.

Science and Common-sense

Before scientific knowledge was popularised people had the knowledge of the events around them. For example a farmer's knowledge about agriculture is inadequate compared to the knowledge of the agricultural scientist. As compared to scientific knowledge common-sense knowledge is shallow, partial, rigid, unsystematic unverified, erroneous, superstitious and sometimes even harmful.

But scientific knowledge is deep, comprehensive, integrated, systematic, verified, exact and hence quite reliable. Differences among the scientists are sorted out through mutual agreement and further experimental testing and evidence whereas common sense opinions are rigid and unverified. There is no growth of common-sense knowledge because of lack of advanced testing procedures involving scientific instruments. Scientific knowledge is *universal* unlike common-sense which is subjective and narrow.

Kinds of Sciences

Sciences such as mathematics are *formal* while some other sciences like physics and chemistry are factual or material sciences. The formal sciences like logic, arithmetics, algebra, and geometry deal with concepts while the physical sciences deal with empirical facts. The formal sciences deal only with logical constructs or concepts. Concepts are not objects or facts of the empirical world. We can notice a vital difference regarding the very nature of statements in physical sciences and formal sciences. Statements of mathematics, etc. are said to be analytical and deductive in nature while statements in empirical sciences are said to be synthetic and inductive in nature. Truth of empirical statements is ascertained from their correspondence with facts. Knowledge of the external world can come only from sense-experience. And hence, sense-experience is the foundation of the claims of sciences.

Questions in Science

There are mysteries in the universe. Perspectives of the scientists about these mysteries are different from those of theologians.

1. What is the universe made of?

It was the Greek philosopher *Thales* who raised the above fundamental question about the universe. He told that the universe is made of water. This enquiry about the constituents of the universe later on evolved into modern day chemistry. To-day the scientists are trying to explain *dark matter* and *dark energy*.

2. How did life begin?

Four billion years age something started stirring in the primordial soup. A few simple chemicals got together and made biology- the first molecules capable of replicating themselves appeared. We humans are linked by evolution to those early biological molecules. But how did the basic chemicals present on early earth spontaneously arrange themselves into something resembling life? How did we get DNA? What did the first cells look like? Some say life began in hot pools of near volcanoes, others that it was kick-started by meteorites hitting the sea.

3. Are we alone in the universe?

Man is curious to find out whether there are living species in other places which are many light years away. In recent years in this regard scientists have tried to explore *Mars*. The next few decades will be an exciting time to be an alien hunter with upto 60 billion potentially habitable planets in our Milky Way galaxy alone.

4. What makes us human?

If we look at the human DNA, it is 99% identical to a chimpanzee's and 50% to a banana's. However we have bigger brains than most animals – not the biggest. A lot of the things we once thought distinguishing about us-language, tool-use, recognizing ourselves in the mirror- are seen in other animals too. According to Henri Bergson the plants have consciousness, but in torpor stage. The animals act *instinctively*; but only human beings have *intellect*. The *instinct* which is self-interested in the animals become disinterested in the humans and called *intuition*.

5. What is consciousness?

We are still unable to define consciousness. Biologists consider consciousness located in different brain regions networked together rather than a single part of the brain. There are still debates going on about the relationship between *mind* and *consciousness*. There are also arguments that there is no such thing as 'mind' and that consciousness is related to the brain and not mind.

6. What are dreams?

Scientists are still searching for a complete explanation of why we sleep and dream. According to Sigmund Freud, the psycho-analyst, the dreams are expressions of unfulfilled wishes (often sexual). Other views suggest that dreams are anything but the random firing of a sleeping brain.

7. Why is these matter?

Cosmologists suggest that the big bang created both

matter and anti-matter and therefore we are in the universe. Theologians opine that God created matter. But the Jain philosophers do not accept that the world was created by God. It is still a mystery how the universe came into existence. Physicists are of the view that there are multiple universes and there are infinite number of universes.

8. What is energy?

We get energy from fossil fuels. But it is also possible to produce energy from solar rays and nuclear fusion machine

9. What are space and time?

10. What are black – holes?

11. What are robots?

12. What are numbers? And

13. Can man be immortal are some of the questions raised in science.

Science and Western Civilisation

The scientific method for relying on evidence – on facts- was one of the supreme achievements of western civilisation. The material wealth and power that stemmed from the codification of the scientific method is exactly why western civilization has been so successful over the last 500 years. The twentieth century saw significant advancements in the practice of medicine, mathematics, and physics; the development of biological taxonomy; a new understanding of magnetism and electricity; and the maturation of chemistry as a discipline, which established the foundations of chemistry. The scientific revolution which emphasized systematic experimentation as the most valid research method, resulted in developments in mathematics, physics, astronomy, biology and chemistry. These developments transformed the views of society about nature.

During the scientific revolution, changing perceptions about the role of the scientist in respect to nature, and the value of experimental or observed evidence, led to a scientific methodology in which empiricism played a large, but not absolute role.

The west has contributed a great many technological, political, philosophical artistic and religious aspects to modern international culture: having been a crucible of Catholicism, protestantism, democracy, industrialization the first major civilisation to seek to abolish slavery during the nineteenth century. Science influences society through its knowledge and world view. Scientific knowledge and the procedures used by scientists influence the way many individuals in society think, about themselves, others, and the environment. The effect of science on society is neither entirety beneficial nor entirely detrimental. Science made human life comfortable through various inventions in science. Cars computers, internet, aeroplanes, ships and many technological achievements helped mankind to have comforts in the society.

Civilisational Crisis in the West

The more there are advances in science and technology, the more we are witnessing material progress in the society. But are we progressing in the right direction? There is change no doubt, but is the change for better or for worse? Why fanaticism, hatred and violence are in the rise while virtues like *toleration* and *non-violence* are not followed in the society? *Mahatma Gandhi* in India and Benedetto Croce in the West were critics of rationality and uncontrolled consumerism. Both Gandhi and Croce were witness to the civilisational crisis of their time, which made them critical of those theories of knowledge which separated the *knower* from the *known, faith* from *reason*. A man of reason and a man of non-violence,

Mahatma Gandhi saw contradictions in the existing theories of knowledge; the rationalists and the empiricists accepted compartmental views of reality. Reason has its limitations as it cannot reconcile fact with value, parts with the whole, outer and the inner. Gandhi thus became a critic of modern western civilisation. For him both reason and faith are necessary for human progress. His experiments with truth made him feel the pulse of reality and to explore the unseen as a shadow of the seen.

Western Civilisation and Ecological Crisis

The ecological crisis has come to be recognized as one of the fundamental problems of the world. A critical awareness of the socio-political structure of the present world is inevitable for understanding the ecological crisis of the present world. An enquiry into ecological problem is inevitably related to the politically and economically sanctioned structures of inequality and domination that contribute to the environmental crisis and its savage effects on human beings. Marx wrote in his capital:

> "The more a country starts its development on the foundations of modern industry like the United States, for example, the more rapid is the process of destruction. Capitalist production, therefore develops technology, and the combination together of various processes into social whole only by sapping the original sources of all wealth-the soil and labourer".

Developmental processes invite our intrusion into ecosystem. "There is no documentation of civilisation which is not at the same time a documentation of barbarism" according to Benjamin. With less than 6 percent of the world's population, the U.S.A. account for 40 percent of annual global consumption of natural resources and for over 40 percent of pollutants in the bio-sphere. There are two major blocs, the G-7 nation and the G-77 nation. The G-7, nation hold about one-fifth of the world's five billion persons and they produce and consume about four fifths of all goods and services.

Proportionate Production and Consumption Among Nations

The development process all over the world, is now under the control of 'Global capital'. The root of most of to-days environmental problems is the disparities between the developed and the under developed nations. Military industrial complex of the capitalist world solely exists for money making. Solution to the ecological crises cannot be resolved without an equally radical transformation of capitalist productive forces. Western civilisation which was the culmination of industrial and scientific revolutions though helped mankind had also created crisis in human values. By subjugating nature and through over exploitation of it, the reverence for nature has been lost. Too-much of material wealth of the west has created the divisions among the developed and developing nations. For the future survival of man, virtues like love, Justice, Equality and Tolerance are essential.

Sciences and Philosophy of Science

Philosophy of science is a part of philosophy, which attempts to do for science what philosophy in general does for the whole of human experience; science aims at explanation, philosophy of understanding. In the history of philosophy there have been fashions of metaphysical speculation and fashions of logical analysis. The difference between science and philosophy of science is one of degree and not of kind. The relations that exist between sense data and science are analogous to those between science and philosophy of science.

Philosophy is generally understood as search for truth. Epistemology, Logic, Ethics and Aesthetics form the part of philosophy. In recent years, absolute objectivity is ascribed to science by some thinkers. The other conception of science is that the 'transcendental entities' are beyond its scope of study. However in modern physics, the concepts such as 'electron' and 'magnetic field' do not restrict science to the study of only empirical phenomena. In *pre-Socratic* thought there was no distinction between philosophy and science. It is only in *Kant,* one finds a non-reductionist distinction between philosophy and science.[1] The Greeks considered science as Enlightenment whereas the function of science according to *Bacon* is to enhance human life. The view of science as absolutely objective and completely removed from the cultural context of the scientist persisted until the second half of the twentieth century. The logical positivists furthered this description of science by establishing scientific statements as paradigm of meaningful language. But the later developments in science had abandoned the logical positivist's position. Apart from objectivity the other norms of science are *empirical validity, logical clarity, logical consistency of the mutual implications of propositions* and *generality of the principles involved.* According to Merton, a sociologist "the ethos of modern science" is guided by four imperatives: Universalism[2], communism[3], disinterestedness[4] and organized skepticism[5]. The sociologist Bern and Barber considers rationality and emotional neutrality as added norms of science.[6]

The logical empiricist or Hypothetico-deductive interpretation of science was challenged by thinkers like Toulmin and Thomas Kuhn. The logical positivists' verifiability principle was rejected by Karl popper. Since for Popper all scientific truths are only provisionally true, the principle of falsification is applied for the statements to be true or false. From the earliest time, the cosmological thought in physical science abstracted and hypostazied form and content of Reality. But the Reality is a compound product of both form and context. Any attempt to separate form from content leads to abstraction[7]. Modern physics devices the distinction between substance and function.[8] There is no static matter (with a certain structure to account for its function) which moves to produce phenomena; matter is what it does, the world is a process to be described by statistical laws and not to be resolved into dead matter and fixed geometrical structure and mechanical laws.

Most people suppose that philosophers think about very general and very deep questions, at the heart of which is the problem of the relation of man to the universe. Philosophy of science would be a discussion of the plan of the scientific enterprise in the whole pattern of life.

Philosophy of science is interpreted as a critique of science. Another interpretation is that it is an inductive metaphysics. The third interpretation is that it is a pragmatic of science. As a critique of science it analysis the language of sciences; the semantics and syntax of scientific language are analysed. As an inductive metaphysics, it uses the inductive method of science, but unlike science it focuses on the transcendental entities also. The key issues in philosophy of science include scientific method, discovery of theory in science, structure and validation of scientific explanation. As pragmatics of science, philosophy of science tries to relate the findings of scientists to the human welfare and upliftment.

Discovery of Theory in Science

Philosophy of science considers the various sciences as finished products of a historical process. The historical order of development is determined by curiosity, accident or the pressure of necessity. Science explains while philosophy tries to understand. All scientific theories can be traceable to the acceptance of four matters of fact:

1. That something exists
2. That something can be known

3. That there is something which matters; and
4. That something makes sense and can be reflected upon.

The above four matters of fact correspond to four branches of Philosophy:

1. Metaphysics (theory of being which deals with what exists)
2. Epistemology (theory of knowledge which deals with what can be known)
3. Axiology (theory of value) and
4. Logic

In the above four matters of fact Epistemology, Metaphysics and Logic are taken for study in Philosophy of science. Since scientific knowledge is *empirical,* there are three problematic steps to be examined:

1. The step from any experience at all to experience of a world of one's own
2. The step from experience of that world to knowledge of it; and
3. The step from knowledge of that world to knowledge of a world in common

In order to understand the transition from experience to knowledge it is necessary that there is a *correlation* between *Perception, thought* and *language.*

There are at least *three different approaches* to the study of Philosophy of science:

1. Logical Empiricism 2. Historical and 3. Aristotelian Natural Philosophy.

The logical empiricists trace their origin to the group of Vienna circle according to whom any statement is valid only if it is empirically *verifiable*. Since metaphysical and ethical statements are not verifiable they are *meaningless*. However later empiricists softened their approach and spoke of *confirmation* rather than *verification*. Rudolf Carnap and Carl Hempel the noted logical empiricists mention at least four problems: 1. 'The theoretician's dilemma' (the problem of the relation between theoretical and observational terms in a scientific explanation). Logic offers the most obvious solution, through the translatability of *theoretical* and *observational* terms. This leads directly to the paradox. Translation would be effected by a *logical equivalence* between two sets of terms; but by clear rules of mathematical logic, this leads to the embarrassing consequence that the equivalence remains true even if the *datum* described by an observational term is not observed. Thus non observation seems to support theoretical terms equally as well as observation.

2. *"Law like statements"*

This is the "problem of counterfactual conditionals". The logical empiricists face difficulty of distinguishing logically between "law like" universal conjunctions and those that are not.

3. *"Explanation – prediction symmetry"*

The 'covering-law' model seems to imply that the explanation is logically the same as prediction of an event after the fact, and prediction is simply explanation before fact.

4. *"The problem of confirmation"*

The modern version of the old logical positivism is the problem of confirmation Carnap's attempt to interpret confirmation led to the theory of probability and problem of induction.

Historical Approach

The logical approach to philosophy of science is challenged by Michael Polanyi according to whom "subjective" and personal interpretations of philosophy of science have more validity than scientific objectivity. He feels that the historical approaches of Hanson and Thomas Kuhn as well as the approaches of Stephen Toulmin, J. Bronowski and Gerald Holton are basically similar to his own view. Kuhn is opposed to the logical-empiricist ideal. He is critical of the logical-empiricist's inquiry about the testing, verification or falsification of established scientific theories. One of his basic conceptions is that "scientific fact and theory are not categorically separable, that in the revolutionary transition from one "paradigm-based" scientific tradition to another, the very empiricist data themselves are "in commensurable". A key to the understanding of Kuhn is what he means by a "paradigm-based scientific tradition"

Aristotle's Natural Philosophy

The third approach to philosophy of science is Aristotle's natural philosophy. Though, other philosophers of science dismiss Aristotle's theory as *naive,* his view remains a possible interpretation of knowledge of the world. The "realist" option "can be summarised in terms of three basic questions faced by Aristotle, as well as the implications of the answers he gave: 1) What makes a changeable being what it is? 2) What is nature? 3) What is change? and 4) Implications and foundations of the special sciences.

According to Aristotle material beings simply cannot exist without the natural changes that belong to them. The world is an interrelated system of bodies all acting on one another and each carrying out its assigned role in the whole.

Natural local motion, natural chemical change and functional processes in biology are for Aristotle the foundations of a realist interpretation of the special sciences of physics, chemistry and the life sciences.

Forms of Reasoning in Science

We study the ideal forms of reasoning in Logic : Actual science is a very complex activity. So it is not surprising that there have been several theories, expressing different ideals of scientific reasoning. In Mendel's Laws, the conclusion is drawn, which is agreed to be a law of nature, and the conclusion is based upon evidence already known. In Kepler's law about the orbit of Mars, the law is already known and is tested by drawing conclusions from the law and testing them by further observations.

Inductive Method

The chief exponents of the Inductive method have been *William of Ockham, John Herschel* and *J.S. Mill*. The inductive laws are also called Mill's canons: a) The method of Agreement and b) The method of Difference.

The Method of Agreement stands on the ground that whatever can be eliminated is not connected with the phenomenon by any law. The method of Difference has for its foundation, that whatever cannot be eliminated is connected with the phenomenon by a law. Through these laws Mill attempted to pass from facts to general laws. Mills canons have been promoted as a complete theory of science. This theory can be expressed in three principles: a) The Principle of Accumulation, b) The Principle of Induction and c) The Principle of Instance Confirmation. However, there are criticisms against Mill's canons.

Doctrine of Falsifiability

If science is not a process of the confirmation by instances of inductively derived laws of nature, perhaps it is a process of *falsification* by instances of conjectures which have no logical basis in the facts hitherto known. This version of inductivism has been developed in modern times by *Karl Popper*. However, Kuhn is critical of the falsification approach to Philosophy of science. For him any discovery of science is related to the social and historical developments.

Positivism

The positivistic ideal of reason is that a theory should have a deductive structure, the ideal form of reasoning in mathematics, i.e. a theory should have the form of a theorem. Prediction and explanation must have the same logical form. Explanation is achieved from a 'covering law'.

Metaphysics is seen as providing a series of options among ways of the thinking; and the choice of option determines to a large extent the kind of philosophy of science that emerges. Therefore metaphysical questions like substance are not irrelevant to philosophy of science. Thinkers like Aristotle Descartes, Spinoza and Leibnitz have contributed to theory of substance. Other areas of philosophy of science include causality, space, time, atomism and evolution. In modem times artificial intelligence, cloning, semiotics have contribute to problems in philosophy of science. Kant's dualism between space and time is based on the dualism between geometry and arithmetic. However, Henri Bergson says time is consciousness. There is no separation between space and time. In modern science Einstein's theory of Relativity of space and time repudiates Newtonianism theory of space and time which is absolutistic. The Chinese believed in cyclic theory of time unlike the linear time of the western thinkers. Philosophy of science takes for study only the western thinker's contribution to the subject. Bertrand Russell in his *History of Western Philosophy* acknowledges the fact that the present *Arab numerals* in Mathematics are the result of the synthesis of *Indian* and *Greek* roots. Apart from mathematics the ancient Indians had thorough knowledge about atomic theory (*Vaisheshika*), evolution (*Sankhya*) astronomy and medicine. However this book focuses mainly on discovery, method and aims of science. Induction, probability, verification, confirmation and explanation in science are the thrust areas for analysis.

References

1. Roy Bhaskar, *The Possibility of Naturalism: A Philosophical Critique of the Contemporary Human Sciences*, The Harvester Press, Sussex, 1978, p. 5.
2. *Universalism*- Truth claims, whatever their source are to be subjected to pre-established impersonal criteria consonant with observation and with previously established knowledge.
3. *Communism*- Scientific knowledge becomes public property and the process of its certification is communal.
4. *Disinterestedness*- Truth seeking is to be valued above personal aggrandisement, and constantly must be subjected to peer accountability.
5. *Organized skepticism*- Temporal suspension of judgment and detached scrutiny of beliefs.
6. William W. Lawrence, *Modern Science and Human Values*, Oxford University Press, New York, 1986, p. 4.
7. P.K. Sengupta (ed.) *Pravas Jivan Chaudhury on Multi-Aspects of Philosophy*, Indian Council of Philosophical Research, New Delhi, 2003, p. 172.
8. *Ibid.*, pp. 181-182.

Chapter III

Induction and Confirmation

Francis Bacon

Francis Bacon is considered as the founder of modern inductive method. He was the pioneer in the attempt at logical systematisation of scientific procedures. In his important book *The Advancement of learning,* his saying:

"Knowledge is power" became popular. He held that philosophy should be kept separate from theology, not intimately blended with it as in scholasticism. He was an advocate of the doctrine of "double truth", that of reason and revelation.

Bacon was the first scientifically minded philosopher who emphasised the importance of induction as opposed to deduction. Like most of his successors, he tried to find some better kind of induction than what is called induction by simple enumeration. Induction by simple enumeration may be illustrated by a parable. There was once upon a time a Census officer who had to record the names of all householders in a certain Welch village. The first that he questioned was called William Williams; so were the second, third, fourth... At last he said to himself; This is tedious; evidently they are all called William Williams. 'I shall put them down so and take a holiday: But he was wrong; there was just one whose name was John Jones. This shows that we may go astray if we trust too implicitly to induction by simple enumeration.

Bacon believed that he had a method by which induction could be made something better than this. He wished for example, to discover the nature of heat, which he supposed to consist of rapid irregular motions of the small parts of bodies. His method was to make lists of hot bodies, lists of cold bodies, and lists of bodies of varying degrees of heat. He hoped that these lists would show some characteristic always present in hot bodies and absent in cold bodies and present in varying degrees in bodies of different degrees of heat. By this method he expected to arrive at general laws, having, in the first instance, the lowest degrees of generality. From a number of such laws he hoped to reach laws of the second degree of generality and so on. A suggested law should be tested by being applied in new circumstances; if it worked in these circumstances it was to that extent *confirmed*. Some instances are specially valuable because they enable us to decide between two theories each possible as far as previous observations are concerned; such instances are called 'prerogative' instances

Bacon not only despised the Syllogism, but emphasized *presuppositionless observation* in his inductive method. He rejected deductive *syllogism* of Aristotle. According to him syllogism is quite useless discovering something new. Hence it was barren of any fruitful result. Besides at the time of Bacon the universal premise in any syllogism could be got from Bible, Aristotle or other authorities. This led to hopeless muddle for anything could be proved or disproved. Therefore Bacon discarded syllogism by comparing it to a consecrated virgin, bearing no fruit Bacon attributed the hopelessness of philosophy to the following causes.

1. The prejudice against experiments and matters of actual facts
2. The blind prejudice and fanaticism of religion which distort and warp judgment
3. The exclusive attention to morals, politics and theology
4. Too much veneration for antiquity
5. Failure to overcome the difficulties arising in the actual investigation of nature

Idolas

As opposed to syllogism Bacon hoped to give a method of investigation a *Novum Organum*. The former philosophy proved hopeless for it based itself on conceptions derived from untested knowledge, merely based on authority. The new method then must be based on experience of fresh facts. Instead of anticipating nature we should interrogate nature in order to wrest from her the secrets known as the laws of nature. But before we hope to get facts from experience, our mind should be free from bias and prejudice. The initial need for a dispassionate enquiry, of nature consists in getting rid of *illusions* or *Idols* which warp and distort our judgement. Bacon points out that there are four kinds of *phantoms* of *idols* which prejudice us in getting the particular fact leading to the discovery of laws. These four idols may be thus enumerated.

1. Idola Tribus

This illusion is the most common one for it is predisposition which more or less besets everyone. For example we read our own ends or purpose in the things of nature and usually judge them in terms of final causes. We look upon trees, flowers and animals from human standpoint, as if they are created for human needs. Thus Bacon anticipates Spinoza in rejecting the teleological explanation of nature.

2. *Idola Specus*

In addition to general bias everybody has some specialised cave or den of his own called Idola specus. These idolas take their rise in the peculiarities of mental or bodily structure, in education, habit or accident. For example, to the jaundiced eye everything appears yellow. This also includes all those prejudices which arise from one-sided devotion to one's own method, profession or society

3. *Idola Fori*

This arises from the connection of words and names. We think that we guide the words, but really in many cases words guide on thoughts. Very many false words arise from their association with false theory. For example, we still say, that the sun set or rises though we do not now believe that the sun moves round the earth.

4. *Idola Theatri*

These illusions arise from the dogmas of philosophers like the dogmas of the sophistical, Empirical and Superstitious systems

a) In sophistical system the dialectic subtleties are used about common experience

b) Empirical generalisation is one which is based on rash and chance observation.

c) In superstitious system the theories of nature are built on a mystical traditions; e.g. stars move in circles.

Critical Evaluation

After rejecting prejudices and subjective notions of observations Bacon emphasises objective method in the investigations of nature. His objective method is also known as inductive method. Although science was what interested Bacon and although his general outlook was scientific, he missed most of what was being done in science in his day. He rejected the Copernican theory. According to him the end of inductive method consists in the discovery of forms of things; it is not clear to us what Bacon meant by forms. Bacon's inductive method is faulty through insufficient emphasis on hypotheses. He hoped that mere orderly arrangement of data would make the right hypothesis, but this is seldom the case. As a rule, the framing of hypothesis is the most difficult part of scientific work. The part played by deduction in science is greater than Bacon supposed. Often, when a hypothesis has to be tested, there is a long deductive journey from the hypothesis to some consequence that can be tested by observation. Usually the deduction is mathematical, and in this respect Bacon underestimated the importance of mathematics in scientific investigation. Bacon was quite right in rejecting simple enumeration. However, J.S. Mill's canons of inductive method was accepted on the basis of induction by simple enumeration. The thing that is achieved by the theoretical organisation of science is the collection of all subordinate inductions into a few that are very comprehensive – perhaps only one. Since comprehensive inductions are confirmed by so many instances that it is thought legitimate to accept, as regards them, an induction by simple enumeration.

The Induction of David Hume

Like Locke and Berkeley, Hume was also an empiricist. His chief Philosophical work was the *Treatise of Human Nature.*

It is divided into three books, dealing respectively with the *understanding, the passion* and *morals*.

His empiricism is revealed in the first book. He begins with the distinction between "impressions" and "ideas". These are two kinds of perceptions of which impressions are those that have more force and violence. By ideas I mean the faint images of these in thinking and reasoning'. Ideas, at least when simple are like impressions, but fainter. Every simple idea has a simple impression, which resembles it; and every impression a corresponding idea. All our simple ideas in their first appearance are derived from simple impressions, which are correspondent to them and which they exactly represent. Complex ideas on the other hand need not resemble impressions. We can imagine a winged horse without having ever seen one. But the constituents of this complex idea are all derived from experience; for example a man born blind has no ideas of colors. Among ideas, those that retain a considerable degree of vivacity of the original impressions belong to memory, the others to imagination. Hume banishes the conception of substance from psychology as Berkeley had banished it from physics. He also rejected Descartes' theory of innate ideas. For Hume there is *no self* of great importance since mind is only a bundle of impressions. No man perceives his own brain, yet, in an important sense he has an idea of it. Such ideas, which are inferences from perception are not logically true. All *psychological* knowledge can be stated without introducing a permanent 'self'. Further, the 'self' as defined can be nothing but a bundle of perception, not a new simple 'thing'. It does not follow that there is no 'self'; it only follows that we cannot know whether there is 'self' or not, and that the 'self' except as a 'bundle' of perceptions cannot enter into any part of our knowledge. This conclusion is important in metaphysics in rejecting any metaphysical entity like 'soul'.

Hume's Rejection of Induction

Hume's views on induction are known in the section called "Of knowledge and Probability" of his *Treatise*. He means probability not in the mathematical sense of throwing dice. What Hume is concerned with is uncertain knowledge, such as is obtained from empirical data by *inferences* that are not demonstrative. This includes all our knowledge as to the future, and as to *unobserved* portions of the past and present. In fact, it includes everything except, on the one hand, direct observation, and on the other, logic and mathematics. The analysis of such 'probable' knowledge led Hume to certain *skeptical* conclusion. He was also called a skeptic. Hume's skeptical view rejected the *uniformity of Nature*. His rejection of uniformity of Nature is closely related to his rejection of induction in science. The movement of sun, moon, earth and other natural phenomena are regulated by cosmic order. If water quenches our thirst to-day we don't doubt that to-morrow water will not quench our thirst. Since Hume as a skeptic questions, the certainty of future events his views on induction are correct as far as he is concerned. Induction is a method of science in which we observe a few cases and make a statement about the future occurrence of an event:

A is mortal

B is mortal

∴ All men are mortal

In the statement "All men are mortal", we have not verified empirically the validity of the term "All". Since, the future occurrences are *unobservable,* Hume was right in holding the view that induction is not a valid method of science.

Hume's Rejection of Causality

According to Hume the *causal* events which are observed

by us are only *psychological* and not logical. In the proposition' A causes B', the two events A and B are merely conjoined together and therefore there is only conjunction of two events by us. When we observed 'clouds' and if there were rains in the past, our mind has the habit of psychologically conjoining both clouds and rains. Therefore when we say 'A causes B', all that we have a *right* to say is that in past experience, A and B have frequently appeared together or in rapid succession, and no instance has been observed of A not followed or accompanied by B. However many instances we may have observed of the conjunction of A and B, that gives *no reason* for expecting them to be conjoined on a future occasion, though it is a *cause* of this expectation, i.e. it has been frequently observed to be conjoined with such an expectation. Mere conjunction of events in the past or induction by enumeration is not a valid form of argument. If Hume's position of *skepticism* is accepted, then the validity of future occurrence of events which are empirical is irrational. Hume is right in his own way in rejecting induction.

Goodman's New Riddle of Induction

Goodman poses *Hume's problem of induction* as a problem of the validity of the predictions we make. Since predictions are about what has yet to be observed and because there is no necessary connection between what has been observed and what will be observed, there is no objective justification for these predictions. Deductive logic cannot be used to infer predictions about future observations based on past observations because there are no valid rules of deductive logic for such inferences. Hume's answer was that observations of one kind of event following another kind of event result in habits of regularity (i.e. associating one kind with another kind). Predictions are then based on these regularities of habits of mind. Goodman takes Hume's answer to be serious one. His view is that Hume has identified something deeper. To illustrate this, Goodman turns to the problem of justifying a *system of rules of deduction*. For Goodman the validity of a deductive system is justified by its conformity to good deductive practice. In the context of justifying rules of induction this becomes the problem of confirmation of generalisations for Goodman.

The new riddle of induction, for Goodman rests on our ability to distinguish *law like* from *non law-like* generalisations. Law-like generalisations are capable of confirmation while *non law-like* generalisations are not. *Law-like* generalisations are required for making predictions. Using examples from Goodman, the generalisation that all copper conducts electricity is a basis for predicting that this piece of copper will conduct electricity. The generalisation that all men in a given room are third sons, however, is not a basis for predicting that a given man in that room is a third son.

The question, therefore, is what makes some generalisations *law-like* and others *accidental*. This for Goodman becomes a problem of determining which predicates are *projectable* (i.e. can be used in law-like generalisation that serve as predictions) and which are not. Goodman argues that this where the fundamental problem, lies. This problem is known as *Goodman's. Paradox:* from the apparently strong evidence that all emeralds examined thus far have been *grue*, one may inductively conclude that all future emeralds will be grue. However, whether this prediction is law like or not depends on the predicates used in this prediction. Hume missed this problem. We do not by habit form generalisations from all associations of events we have observed but only some of them. Goodman's solution is to argue that law-like predictions are based on projectable predicates such as *grue* and *bleen* and not on non-projectable predicates such as *bleen* and *grue* and what makes predicates projectable is their *entrenchment*, which depends on their successful past projections. Thus *grue* and *bleen* function in Goodman's arguments to both illustrate the new riddle of induction and to illustrate the distinction between projectable and non-projectable Predicates.

Does Induction make science possible?

Laws in science are arrived at through scientific method which has the following stages: 1) Observation 2) Collection of data 3) Hypothesis and 4) Law.

The observation of an empirical phenomena may be driven by man's curiosity, necessity, accident or by programming. If there is a kind of regularity of occurrences of two events A and B, the former preceding the later, man says that A causes B. If there is a kind of necessary relationship between A and B, he concludes that whenever A occurs, B also occurs. Therefore induction is a method used in science to frame a scientific hypothesis after observing some cases. In Induction we go from particulars to universals. "All bodies gravitate" is a statement arrived at by Newton after repeated observation of physical objects falling on the ground. Similarly "All men are mortal" is valid though it is not possible to verify the mortality of future generation of men. The degree of validity of inductive generalisations lies in the fact that the number of cases of observations must be more. The more number of observations increase the validity of induction as a method of science. We cannot jump to a conclusion after observing some cases. Therefore inductive generalisations lead only to probable statement unlike in deductive statements. In deductive method we find a logical necessity between *premises* and *conclusions*. But in inductive method explanation of an event arrived at through inductive generalisation is *only probable* and not certain.

Critical Evaluation of Induction

Induction as a valid method of science has been questioned by many scholars: Francis Bacon, David Hume,

Goodman Karl Popper, Kuhn, Lakatos, Feyeraband and Noam Chomsky.

Bacon finds fault with induction on the ground that in the very process of observation of events man has prejudices. Induction is possible only when there is presuppositionless observation which is very unlikely. As a skeptist Hume rejects any kind of causality and according to him man takes *uniformity of Nature* for granted. Hume questions the uniformity of Nature and hence just because there were past occurrences of events there is no guarantee that in future too there will be such occurrences. Goodman distinguishes between law – like and non-law-like generalisations in science.

In induction there is often no such distinction and hence induction as a valid method is questioned by Goodman. According to Popper there is no permanent scientific theory. All Scientific theories are *provisionally* true which can be falsified. Kuhn also supports Popper in declaring that there are no permanent scientific theories. Social context determine scientific theories. As paradigm change in society scientific theories also will change accordingly. Feyeraband is very critical of scientific method. He argues that observation of facts, the very first step of scientific method is very often neither impartial nor really objective. Moreover, establishing a general proposition on the basis of particular instances is all unwarranted. To stick to one method is wrong even if it is scientific method.

Lakotas advocates a Research Programme approach. He says in science anything, goes. According to him the common man is fooled by the show of scientists who very often follow their own subjective wishes. Such words as scientific laws, causation, qualities, powers, and potentialities of the objective facts are subjective projections of the scientists.

Noam Chomsky finds fault with science on the ground

that scientism is an unwarranted claim, because epistemological query which leads to sciences, is only one part of our mental activity and scientism not only neglects the other equally important claims of affective activities, it even means to suppress them. Science is not the whole of life. Science is a good servant, but a bad master. Chomsky even questions the very claim of science as an agency of giving knowledge. He point out that novels can gives us more knowledge about the nature of people than what science does. Science may solve a few problems here and there but it cannot solve the basic mysteries of nature. Even Darwin does not explain much. Hence he rejects scientism based on induction root and branch.

Kuhn says that scientists work in fixed frames and do not question fundamentals and hence they become *one more religion*. Science is concerned only with the ontological side of our life. It leaves the aesthetic life completely untouched.

In spite of the above criticisms against science based on induction it is a fact that science adds huge resources for making human life qualitatively better. It has increased the length, breadth and depth of human life.

CHAPTER IV

LOGICAL POSITIVISM AND SCIENCE

Positivism as a philosophical trend is derived from radical empiricism. According to the programme of logical positivism elaborated by the *Vienna circle,* science begins with the observation of single facts. Established facts provide a basis or initial empirical generalisations which, after an additional study of separate phenomena and events, are transformed into broader generalisations. Universality of statements can only be attained at a theoretical level and such universal truths are regarded as empirical laws constituting the basis and the core of all theoretical knowledge. The development of science thus consists in the progressive expansion of empirical generalisations, and inductive conclusion turns out to be the main instrument of such development.

There is always relationship between empirical experience and theoretical concepts. Their relationship is evident in the history and logic of science. One of the *aims* of logical positivism is to *lay foundation* for science. It advanced an extensive programme providing for a logical restructuring of the whole edifice of science in order to standardise the language of science. Philosophy of science as the logic of science analyses science with the help of mathematical logic.

The other aim of logical positivism is to eliminate metaphysics. According to logical Positivism both ethical and metaphysical statements are meaningless. Since the transcendental entities of metaphysics are beyond sense-perception they cannot be verified. The statements of metaphysics therefore cannot be verified. Therefore the twin aims of logical positivism are 1) to lay foundation for science and 2) to reject metaphysics.

Logic

Logic is the study of the canons or principles of correct reasoning. To discover logical principles from the study of examples we need to be able to recognise when a piece of reasoning is correct. The study of logic will enable us to say why some piece of reasoning is correct or incorrect. However, once the principles of logic have been extracted from examples it is inevitable that they should be used as canons, that is to express the standards to which reasoning should conform. The principle of correct reasoning which holds good for mathematics will not hold good for subjects like chemistry which is an empirical subject. The written expression of scientific knowledge ideally takes the form of a reasoned and systematic exposition. Conclusions will be backed up by reasons. Hypotheses will be considered with respect to the balance of favorable and contrary evidence. Certain logical relationships hold between conclusions and the reason for conclusions. Other logical relationships hold between hypothesis and the reasons which call for their rejection or modification. Relationships such as these are the stuff of logic.

They must conform to the canons or principles of correct reasoning. Some considerations do support a conclusion. Others do not. Judgements on such matters as these express the logical commentary upon the discourse. Logical principles must he produced to back them up.

Logic and Science

In the philosophy of science one branch of philosophical study cannot be studied in isolation with other branch of Philosophy. The study of logic is therefore related to the study of science. The statements describing the evidence will be particular statements of the form: 'In this experiment, when light passed from one medium to another the sine of the angle of incidence bore the same ratio to the sine of the angle of refraction as it did in the other experiments I have done'. The law will be expressed in a quite *general* statement: 'In all cases of the passage of light from one medium to another the sine of the angle of incidence will bear a constant ratio to the sine of the angle of refraction'.

$$\mu = \frac{\sin i}{\sin r}$$

μ - refractive index

i- angle of incidence

r -angle of refraction

This law of refraction in the propagation light is quite general. But deductive logic does not sanction an inference from particular to general. So to speak of *inferring* the law from the evidence is misleading, since it tempts us to think that the law is a conclusion, drawn from particular premises according to some principles of logic. If the principles of deductive logic do not govern the extraction of laws from observation then we cannot say that the truth of laws follows, with logical rigour.

In this case we can say that we can have *belief* in the law and not the *knowledge* of the law. Knowledge is possible only when there is no logical problem. In the same way we can have beliefs about the astronomical facts and beliefs in the future evolution of the world. But these beliefs do not stand the logical scrutiny.

Realism and Science

According to George Berkeley, "To be is to be perceived" (*Esse est percipi*). Berkeley's subjective idealism does not accept the independent existence of the external world. Realism on the other hand accepts the independent existence of the external world like science. In accepting a reality of the external world realism is closely related to science. Realism as a school of thought developed in Britain and America. The two chief forms of realism prevalent in Britain and America are neo-realism and critical realism, each of which acquires slightly different forms in different thinkers. The main point of difference between these two forms consists in their different replies to the epistemological question, whether the object *perceived* is numerically identical with the *object*. Neo-realism answers this question in the affirmative, holding that the two are one. This view is, therefore known as *epistemological monism*. Critical realism answers the question in the negative, holding that the objet perceived and the object existing are two different entities. This theory is known therefore as epistemological dualism. G.E. Moore, Alexander, and Russell are the pioneers of Neo-Realism. Durant Drake, Arthur O. Lovejoy, James Bissett Pratt, Arthur K. Rogers, George Santayana, Roywood Sellars and C.A. Strong jointly presented *Critical Realism*.

Instrumentalism

Among the American Philosophers, Dewey gave a new kind of interpretation to realism which is called *Instrumentalism*- John Dewey's *Pragmatism*. According to John Dewey, Truth is that which works. Many realists viewed mind as a passive recipient of knowledge. But not so Dewey. He is not a passive onlooker at the world. He looks at things not as objects of mere perception and enjoyment but as tools, as *instruments*, and plans for future prospects. For Russell, facts cause our knowledge to be true, whereas for Dewey satisfactory type of *consequences* make our knowledge true. This is why Dewey defines truth on pragmatic lines. For him thinking is always purposive. Hence his theory can be called an intentional theory of knowledge. All progress, all evolution goes on because of new problems. Real learning is by doing. Dewey developed a new kind of education for which he is very famous. Every knowledge is an instrument to serve some need or other. No knowledge is final. Inquiry, perpetual Inquiry, and perpetual manipulation of the relevant factors are the distinct symbols of Dewey's *instrumentalism*. Knowledge is not a goal, but only an instrument to achieve this or that goal.

Empiricism

Why do we believe what we believe to be true? Is our knowledge based on our experience, or is our knowledge based on what others have told us? There are a number of philosophical beliefs about life and experience. Some Philosophies suggest that knowledge must be proven, while other philosophies suggest that it is based on reasoning.

Empiricism is an important part of the scientific method because theories and hypotheses must be observed and tested to be considered accurate. Empiricists tend to be skeptical that anything can be known for certain and, therefore; they tend not to believe in dogmas or absolute truths. This is in contrast to rationalists, who tend to believe that the universe has absolute laws that can be determined and that the human mind is naturally predisposed to understanding certain truths.

Empiricism is a philosophical belief that states that our knowledge of the world is based on our experiences, particularly our *sensory* experiences. According to empiricists, our learning is based on our observations and perception; knowledge is not possible without experience. There are three types of empiricism: classical empiricism, radical empiricism, and moderate empiricism.

Classical Empiricism

Classical empiricism is based on the belief that there is no such thing as innate or in-born knowledge. John Locke is one of the most well-known empiricists; he claimed the mind is a *tabula rasa,* or blank slate, at birth. Locke asserts that our experience of the world provides us with knowledge.

Radical Empiricism

It stems from the belief that our knowledge of the world is based solely on our senses; if something is not experienced through our senses, it does not exist according to radical empiricist. Radical empiricists reject religious beliefs because such beliefs cannot be investigated through the evidence of the senses.

Moderate Empiricism

It accepts that some truths (conceptual truths, mathematical truths, logical truths) are justified and known independent of sense-experience.

Rationalism and Empiricism

a) Empiricism believes that knowledge is derived from experience/ experimentation whereas rationalism believes that knowledge is derived from logic and reason.

b) For empiricism *experimental science* is the *paradigm* of knowledge whereas rationalism believes that *mathematics* is the paradigm of knowledge.

c) Empiricism believes that experimental science cannot produce *certainty* whereas rationalists believe that genuine knowledge is certain because it is *rational, not empirical*.

Empiricism of Hume

David Hume was critical of rationalism and argued that *inductive reasoning* and beliefs in *causality* cannot be justified. We never actually perceive that one event causes another but only experience the *"constant conjunctions"* of events. The problem of induction means that to draw any causal inference from past experience it is necessary to presuppose that the future will resemble the past, a presupposition which cannot itself be grounded in prior experience. He was a *sentimentalist* and argued that human behavior is governed by *passions* and not by *reason*. He denied *self* and held the view that we experience only a *bundle of sensations* and the self is nothing but more than this bundle of causally connected perceptions. Hume influenced *utilitarianism, logical positivism, philosophy of science,* early analytic philosophy, cognitive science and many other fields. Immanuel Kant credited Hume as the inspiration who had awakened him from his *"dogmatic slumbers"*. Hume's problem of induction was fundamental importance to the philosophy of *Karl Popper*. In his autobiography Popper wrote, "Knowledge is objective; and it is hypothetical or conjectural. This way of looking at the problem made it possible for me to reformulate Hume's problem of induction. This insight resulted in Popper's major work, *The Logic of Scientific Discovery*. In his *conjectures and Refutations,* he wrote: "I approached the problem of induction through Hume. Hume, I felt, was perfectly right in pointing out that induction cannot be logically justified".

Immanuel Kant though was influenced by Hume, rejected Hume's skepticism and for him the "forms of intuition" structure all *experience,* and therefore *"things-in-themselves"* exist. However the experience of the *objects* and *things in themselves* are different. The latter cannot be known whereas the former can be known. The objects of experience are mere *appearance*. Kant developed a theory of experience in which he tried to answer the question whether *synthetic a prior* knowledge is possible which would in turn make it possible to determine the limits of *metaphysical* inquiry. According to him the objects of the senses must conform to our spatial and temporal forms of *intuition*, and that we can consequently have a priori cognition of the objects of the senses. He attempted to explain the relationship between reason and human experience and synthesized both *rationalism* and *empiricism*.

Empiricism and Science

Philosophy of Science has traditionally concentrated its attention on epistemology and logic. Since science means knowledge (from the Latin "Scire", to know) Bertrand Russell claimed, "what science cannot discover mankind cannot know". Knowledge is an ability rather than a possession.

The *origin* of most of this knowledge is *empirical* experience and therefore there are three problematic steps to be examined:

i) The step from any experience at all to experience of a world of one's own.

ii) The step from experience of the world to knowledge of it and

iii) The step from knowledge of that world to knowledge of a world in common.

Perception

In order to understand the transition from experience to knowledge, it is necessary to put oneself in a position of experiencing. For this purpose Edmund Husserl recommended a process called "bracketing"; this means forgetting all that one has learned in order to take an unprejudiced look at what is presented. Phenomenologically, by the objects perceived are "intentional objects". The world of phenomena reveals the properties, configurations, processes, sequences, etc. of the objects of perception.

Thought

Thought is a mechanism for the synthesis of a full world out of the bits and pieces of experience. It is regarded as a second convenient hypothesis (the external world was the first). Concepts are a set of hypothetical entities which correspond to percepts. Concepts are function through *recognition, identification* and *representation*. Concepts have ontological status. They also evoke a habit of expectations. They are functional entities.

Language

Any language has the following three essential ingredients:

i) The sign
ii) The thing of which it is the sign and
iii) The person to whom it is a sign of that thing or in other words, sign, object and interpreter

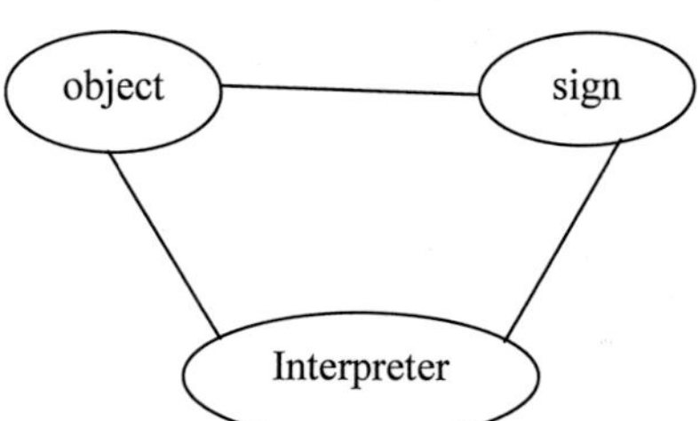

One of the functions of sign is communication. If more than one interpreter is assumed and if every interpreter interprets the sign in the same way, then they share whatever meaning it is that the sign conveys. The language of science has its own special vocabulary referring to particular kinds of object and process. A language which is being used to talk about the world is called an *object language*. The language which we use to discuss this first language is then called a *metalanguage*. For instance, the sentence, "The sentence 'Copper Sulphate is soluble is true" is a metalinguistic philosophic remark mentioning a scientific sentence (belonging to the object language) which actually says something about Copper Sulphate.

Science aims at the development of concepts which will stand for any individual in a particular class, on the assumption that there is a similarity between the members of the class which entails a similarity in their behavior under similar circumstances. Aristotle used his Philosophical concept of *matter* and *form* to classify animals and plants into *species* and *genus*. We may distinguish different senses of similarity in descending order of usefulness for purposes of classification:

i) *Genetic* similarity, i.e. that is between objects having similar origins.

ii) *Structural* similarity, i.e. between objects having similar constituent parts or similar relations between their parts.

iii) Functional similarity, i.e. between objects having similar behavior. Concepts in science are used with clearly *defined* meanings

The correlation of Perception, Thought and Language

The correlation between perception, thought and language can be understood from the following diagram

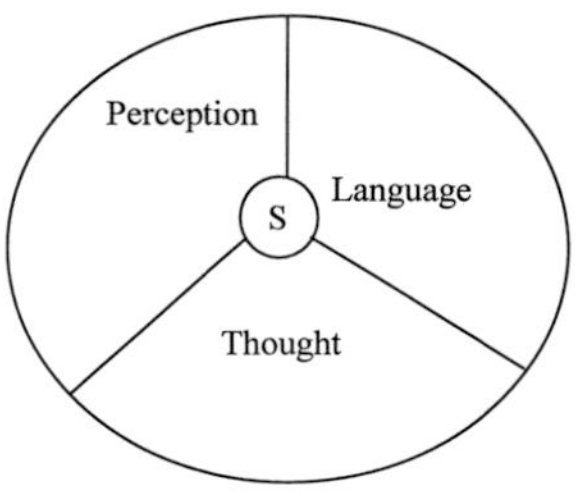

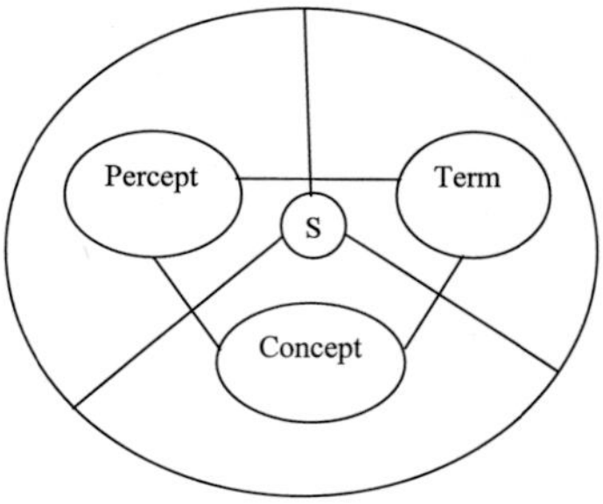

The circumference of the large circle corresponds to the edge of objectivity. There will be *isomorphism* between the three segment if there are corresponding concepts and terms for the percepts

i) If there are corresponding concepts and terms for the percepts.

ii) If there are corresponding percepts and concepts for the terms.

iii) If there are corresponding terms and percepts for the concepts.

In the correlation of perception, thought and language the following kinds of relations are relevant:

a) Logical and grammatical relations in language.

b) Spatial and temporal relations in perception, and whatever psychological theory calls for in thought.

Generalisations, Hypotheses, Laws, Principles and Theory

Generalisations and Hypotheses

A scientist records his observation through a protocol sentence which asserts that something is in fact the case. A protocol sentence can be reached after a finite number of observations and it must be *inter-subjectively corroborated.* Suppose a series of observations are made and every observation is recorded:

This A is B

This A_1 is B

....

Therefore A_n is B

Men have a tendency in such situations to jump from the collection of singular sentences about A A_1, A_2... to a universal statement about the class of A'_s: *All A's are B*. Such a jump is called *generalisation,* and the sentence which results from it will be called *empirical generalisation*. But sometimes in science sentences which are neither observational nor grammatical are also protocol sentences.

Consider for example the sentence

The mass of the electron is 9.107 x 10^{-28} gms. The truth of this sentence rests on the observability of the electron; but the electron is only inferential entity and not observable. Though electrons are not observable, they cause tracks in cloud chambers and on Photographic plates which can be observed. Unlike empirical generalisations, sentences about such unobservable objects are invulnerable in the face of contrary sentences. So, the sentences about electrons are given the status of *hypothesis*. Hypothesis always contain theoretical terms, since any universal sentence containing only observation terms would necessarily have a protocol type sentence for its contradictory. Not all sentences containing theoretical terms, or propositions about theoretical constructs, are hypotheses — only those from which empirical generalisations follow. The truth or falsity of a sentence does not affect its logical classification, and tests of truth or falsity on empirical grounds don't belong to logic. A hypothesis may become a generalisation through the refinement of techniques of observation. Generalisations emerge naturally after a number of particular observations. Every sentence of science falls into one or another of these categories: Protocol sentences, empirical generalisations or hypotheses. All *generalisations* accepted as *true* have the status of *laws,* and all *hypotheses* accepted as true have the status of *principles.*

Ex. The law of conservation of energy is a hypothesis accepted as true since energy is not observed, but rather the penetration of bullets is observed.

Principles are hypotheses accepted as suitable starting points for theoretical work.

A principle turns into a law if what before could not be observed becomes observable by virtue of some advances in experimental technique. A *theory* is a set of universal propositions asserted by means of a corresponding set of universal sentences. These are *isomorphic* with one another. Since scientists form a changing population and are comparatively short-lived beings theory is constantly changing: new laws are discovered, old ones discarded or forgotten. Scientific theory, finally constitutes a particular outlook on the world. The term comes from the Greek 'theories' 'to look at'; scientific theory means knowledgeable outlook. There are other outlooks of the world also apart from the scientific outlook of the world.

Scientific Method

Scientific method means different things to different scientists. According to Plato good theory leads automatically to good practice. The application of this maxim in the present case is simple; if it is understood what the structure of scientific theory is, how it is linked to observation, what steps are necessary in order to confirm a given theory, and so on, then the method of science will be in working toward that structure, establishing those links, and taking those steps. In the present case this will amount to following the pattern of hypotheses, deduction and test. Theories are like maps in geography which guide the traveler to go from one town to another town. As there are different modes of transport from one place to another there can be different methods of arriving at truth in science (though at present the scientists prefer the method of pattern of Hypotheses-deduction-test).

Bacon, Galileo and Descartes propounded an *inductive method* to establish what we would consider epistemological links between hypotheses and instances. Galileo comes closest to the contemporary concept of method in specifying three steps through which a theory has to pass. Galileo's method anticipates the modern methodology of the scientists. His three steps are *intuition, demonstration* and *experiment* which can be translated almost exactly into our terminology, once again as *hypothesis, deduction* and *test*. The greatest advantage of methodological formulations is that they make quite clear the relative importance of the various steps in the epistemological process, regarded as the emergence of a more or less accurate theory from primitive observation and conjecture.

A theory in science has *historical* background. For example *celestial mechanics* has developed over the centuries. The primitive observations and conjectures were provided by *Aristarchus* who as early as the fourth century BCE hit upon the idea that *the earth might possibly go around the sun*. But the idea was rejected by Ptolemaic astronomy. The hypothesis of Aristarchus was taken up by *Copernicus*; but Copernicus could not get enough data to establish the hypothesis. *Brahe* and *Kepler* made further observations and Kepler arrived at the three laws of planetary motion. However, it was left to Newton to axiomatise all this into a system of mechanics in which particular behavior of the heavenly bodies was only a special case of something completely general. Each scientist is responsible for one important stage in the development of theory:

I Aristarchus and Copernicus - Hypothesis

II Brahe - Observational basis

III Kepler - Inductive generalisation

IV Newton - Axiomatic and deductive organization of the finished theory

Each theory in science has its own historical development as the theory of celestial mechanics shows in the above. It is worth distinguishing between two senses in which "method" may be understood - as referring to *methodological application* of standard results, which is the way in which science as an effective body of knowledge enters into the lives of ordinary men, or by as referring to methodological inquiry about the adequacy and reliability of explanations, which is part of philosophical criticism of science as an intellectual activity. The latter sense is relevant in the validation of theory as a method for the tying down of abstract logical systems to empirical contents.

Logical Positivism

The Origins of Movement

Logical Positivism also called logical empiricism as a

movement was organised into a group called the *Vienna circle.* The prominent members of this group were *Moritz Schlick, Otto Neurath* and *Rudolf Carnap.* At Oxford A.J. Ayer popularised the movement. In America E. Nagel and Morris supported the movement. The official Programme on which the Vienna circle was organised had two principal aims:

1) To provide a secure foundation for the sciences.
2) To demonstrate the meaninglessness of metaphysics.

The Conception of Meaning

The Positivists' conception of meaning was first developed by *Ludwig Wittgenstein* in his treatise *Tractatus Logico-Philosophicus.* According to it language is the symbolic representation of facts experienced. It can be analysed into significant assertions called propositions. Every elementary proposition is a picture of some atomic fact experienced. For *Wittgenstein* "the sense of a proposition is a method of its verification". The verification theory of meaning disagreed from the positivists of Vienna circle. However this method demonstrated the meaninglessness of metaphysics and clarified the propositions of science. Wittgenstein changer his position in his later works.

The Elimination of Metaphysics

By metaphysics the positivists mean theory of reality lying beyond experience. The fundamental postulate of metaphysics is that there is a super phenomenal reality like God, soul, etc. Significant propositions or *protocol statements* must correspond to the facts experienced. Since the statements of metaphysical entities cannot be verified empirically such of those statements are meaningless. The method adopted to reject metaphysics is to *analyse* the language of metaphysical statement. There are two sources that give rise to meaningless sentences. *Either* the component words of a sentence lack meaning and the sentences as a whole becomes nonsensical (Ex. Twas brillig and the Slithy toves) or it may be that the constituent words are all individually capable of expressing meanings in other contexts, but in this particular context the words taken together do not yield any sense:

Ex:

1. Caesar is a prime Number.
2. Quadratic equations attend races. Metaphysicians propound the first kind of non-sense.

Role of Philosophy as Logical Analysis of Sciences

The proper functions of Philosophy is to analyse the statements asserted by scientists. The analysis of linguistic expressions of science is called *logic of science* by Rudolf Carnap. This consists of two branches:

1) Logical Syntax

Logical Syntax analyses complex and compound sentences into simple ones. It also investigates the logical relations of consistency and inconsistency, dependence and independence among different sentences.

2) Semantics

Semantic analysis of the language of science focuses on the *meaning* aspect of the sentence. In other words the *syntax* of language indicates the *structure* of a language whereas *semantics* deals with the *meaning* aspect of a language. The clarification, interpretation and co-ordination of the results of the sciences through logical analysis constitute a very useful and worthy programme which philosophy can legitimately pursue.

The Re-interpretation of Science

In their attempts to re-interpret science the logical

positivists make use of concepts such as *probability* from their perspective. Similarly the concepts of induction and laws of nature are also related to theory of verification. There are three different theories advanced by different positivists:

1) Hans Reichenbach holds that owing to variations and errors of observation no assertion can be said to be unconditionally true or false, but can only be probable. Probability lies between absolute truth and absolute falsity. According to this theory no conclusion follows from any premise with absolute certainty, the latter can only imply the former to some degree of probability. Against this theory the chief objection is that it is self contradictory to deny an absolute standard of truth and at the same time speak of the unreliability of observation due to variation.

2) R. Von Mises advocates frequency theory of probability. According to this theory, probability can be asserted on statistical observations and computation. This theory is applicable only in cases of phenomena which can be regarded as members of classes or groups, not as individuals. The third conception of probability is supported by Wittgenstein and Waismann. In this view probability is a kind of logical *relation obtaining between two propositions*. Between any two propositions P and Q there may be three kinds of logical relations. Using *Euler's* circle these may be shown as follows:

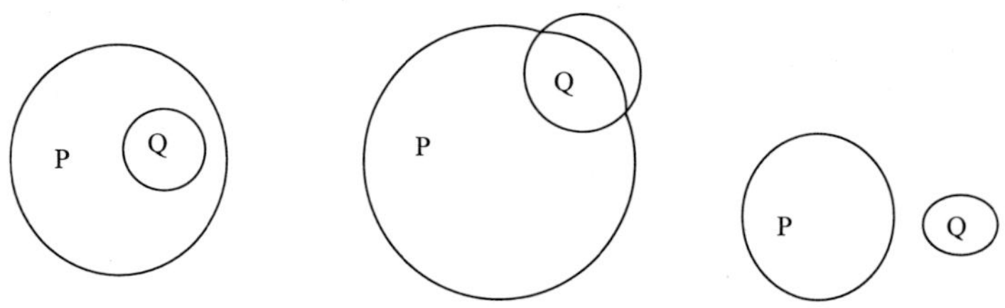

I II III

In the first case P includes Q and Q follows from P (*Entailment*) Ex. All things are human and All kings are animate

In the second Case P neither entails nor excludes Q, P partially overlaps Q. This kind of logical relation between two propositions is called *probability*

Eg. All kings are human and

All kings are fallible.

In the third case P excludes Q. The relation between the two is *contradiction*

Eg. All kings are human and

All kings are inanimate.

3) J.M. Keynes advocates this conception of probability. In this conception probability is not a subjective belief.

Like probability induction is also considered by the positivists from their point of view. The principle of induction is prescriptive injunction to choose those laws which enable us to predict successfully with greatest ease and to describe with the maximum, simplicity. But the laws of science should not be taken to possess any *existential* import. Morris describes in a comprehensive manner, the functions of the *Philosophy of Language* along three directions which he calls *pragmatics, semantics* and *syntactics*. These three branches are called collectively *semiotics*. Sense data which are mental are relative to solipsism in empirical experience. To avoid solipsism, Neurath considered sense-data as the "physiological processes of brain". This behaviorist attitude of Neurath influened Carnap to frame *physicalism* in science.

Critical Estimate of Logical Positivism

The verification theory of meaning is foundational to logical positivism. Hence the critics of logical positivism point out the defects of this theory. If we follow the principle of verification, is it possible to understand the meaning of statements about objects, not yet perceived or of historical statements about the past, or of statements about other minds or about interperceptual states of physical objects, none of which can ever be actually observed? There are statements, the verification of which is not possible:

1) There is mountain on the other side of the moon
2) Arsenic is poisonous
3) This copper wire conducts electricity
4) Man is mortal.

However the logical positivists defend their theory by maintaining that the above statements can be verified *indirectly*. In other words in this case the verification is in the weak sense,

Critics of logical Positivism point out the defects of the *conception of meaning*. It is arbitrary to make meaning *dependent* on *verification*.

A *story* sentence like "a king had four sons" is not dependent on verification and still it has meaning. The logical positivist however admit that there are certain sentences the meaning of which indicate *logical implications*.

Ex. 1. Marriage means responsibility

2. Fear means weakness

Another criticism against positivistic criterion is that it renders its own basic assertions meaningless. The statement, for example, that the meaning of a proposition is the method of its verification is nonsensical as it does not assert any experienceable fact, nor is it reducible to simple factual propositions, nor does it imply any matter of fact which can be observed to verify its truth.

Again this school sets out the express intention of justifying and serving science but gradually it finds it impossible to defend science consistently with its basic principles, and it begins to re-interpret and reform science to suit its principles.

CHAPTER V

THE ROLE OF RATIONALITY IN SCIENCE

Logic is the attempt to specify the rules of correct reasoning, where reasoning is typically a passage of thought from some given or assumed statements to others. The complexity of science is evidenced by the number and diversity of ideal forms of reasoning that have been advocated.

Reasoning from the History of Science

1) Mendel's Laws

These laws describe the ratios of the numbers of individuals which in successive generations of adult plants and animals show certain characteristics. For instance, the children of *brown* eyed *man* and *blue* eyed woman will all have brown eyes, but if one of those children marries someone from a similar background, then the chances are that in every four children of such marriages three will be brown-eyed and one blue-eyed. Mendel formulated general laws which described such cases, where dominant (brown eyes) and recessive (blue byes) 'genetic factors' are grouped in various combinations in people, animals and plants. Mendel reached his laws by reasoning from evidence. This process of reasoning begins with the experimental evidence and passes to the law as conclusion. This is an example for inductive method in science

2) *Hypothetico Deductive Method*

Kepler arrived at the *elliptical* orbit of planets. His theory was that he reached the conclusion first which he considered as hypothesis. Later experimental evidence proved his conclusion to be true. This is Hypothetico-deductive method in science.

3) *Mill's Canons*

a) The Canon of Agreement

If two or more instances of the phenomenon under investigation have only one circumstance in common, the circumstance in which alone all the instances agree is the case (or effect) of the given phenomenon.

b) The Canon of Difference

If an instance in which the phenomenon under investigation occurs, and an instance in which it does not occur have every circumstance in common save one, that one occurring only in the former, the circumstance in which alone the two instances differ is the effect, or the cause, or an indispensable part of the cause of the phenomenon.

Mill's canons are only some among the forms of reasoning, and that they are not capable of proof.

4) *Inductivism*

The idea that something like Mill's Canon exhausts the possibilities of scientific method has been made into a complete philosophy of science, *inductivism.*

Its principles are as follows

a) The principle of Accumulation: that scientific knowledge grows additively by the discovery of independent facts

b) The principle of Induction: that there exists a form of inference by which laws can be inferred from particular facts.

c) The principle of Instance Confirmation: that our degree of belief in the truth of law is proportional to the number of favorable instances of the law.

5. Popper's Doctrine of Falsifiability

If science is not a process of the confirmation by instances of inductively derived laws of nature, perhaps it is a process of falsification by instances of conjectures which have no logical basis in the facts hitherto known. This version of inductivism has been developed by Karl Popper.

6. Positivism

The positivist ideal of reason is that a theory should have a deductive structure, the ideal form of reasoning in mathematics, i.e. a theory should have the form of a theorem. Predictions and explanations have the same logical form.

Explanation is achieved by deduction of what is to be explained from a 'covering-law', together with ancillary premises. Inductivism, falsificationism and positivism each express one of a complex of useful forms of reasoning.

Popper's Doctrine of Falsifiability

Popper's falsifiability theory retains the inductive picture of laws of nature as general statements of correlations among phenomena, and evidence as particular statements of correlations among observables. Popper's radical proposal is that evidence is valuable only in so far as it would tend to falsify general statements. Apiece of evidence that would usually be regarded as favourable and supporting a hypothesis is treated by Popper, at least in some of his work, rather as an instance of the failure of an attempt to falsify the hypothesis under test. Popper refers to this view of evidence as the Radical Principle. He uses the Radical Principle to classify hypotheses as either empirical or non-empirical and non-scientific. Such of those statements which can be falsified by empirical evidence are scientific and those statements which cannot be empirically falsified by tests are non-scientific. Reasoning by analogy according to popper has no advantage over guess-work. The Radical Principle of Popper demands a radical reinterpretation of most scientific work, since all evidence which was supposed to be favourable to a hypothesis is now to be treated as an attempt at falsification that has failed since on this theory logical relations exist only between falsificatory evidence and hypotheses, no logical relations can exist between favourable evidence and hypotheses. The following two, classes of statements are called non-scientific:

1) There are molecules

   - Existential statement

2) The probability that this die will come up 6 at the next throw is 1:6

   - Probability statement

The first statement is non-scientific because they are unfalsifiable.

The second statement is non-scientific because the failure of the dice to come up 6 in that throw or even in the next six throws does not count as evidence strong enough to falsify the statement.

However Popper's falsification theory has drawbacks.

1) It confuses psychological conditions for science with logical conditions.
2) Popper's rejection of existential statements is unacceptable. In fact the existential statements act as framework for the changing hypotheses. Therefore existential statements are not non-scientific.
3) The intellectual process by which hypotheses are discovered and theories formulated are capable only of psychological studies and there is no rational process of discovery in science. Therefore falsifiability cannot be considered as a unique ideal of reason.

Scientific Inference or Deduction

Aristotle's Principles of reasoning is relevant to scientific inference or deduction. It can be summed up in the traditional square of opposition. General statements can be either affirmative, 'All metals are conductors' or negative, 'No metals are conductors'. Either could be a law of nature. The results of experiments could be expressed as 'some metals are conductors' when the experiments have been successful, or 'some metals are not conductors' when the attempt to test some metals for conductivity failed. The relation between these four statements can be shown in a diagram:

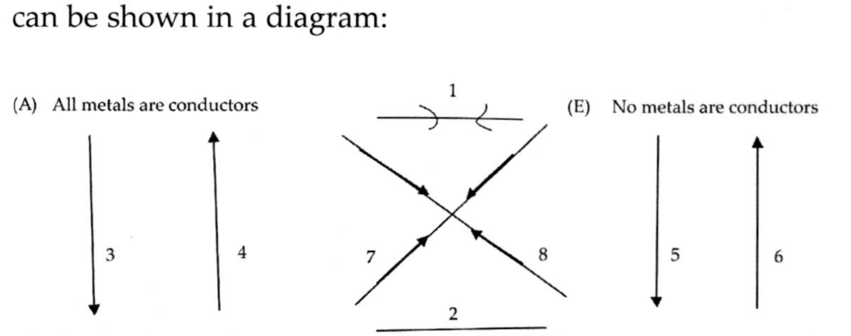

The relations are :

1 A and E cannot be true together

2 I and O cannot be false together

3 and 5 If A is true then so is I. If E is true then so is O

4 and 6 The truth of I supports A, and of O supports E

7 and 8 The truth of I contradicts E and the truth of O contradicts A.

Thus 7 and 8 are the relations that contrary evidence has to hypotheses, while 4 and 6 are the weaker relations that favourable evidence, has to hypotheses. The consequence of Popper's restriction of the logic of science to 3, 5, 7 and 8 is the view that the process of the generation of hypotheses is not one which proceeds according to Popper, in a cloud of conjectures about how things go on. The work of the experimentalists and their results falsify certain of its components.

Demarcation between Science and Non-science

According to the 'verification version' of logical positivism, the criterion of the scientific value of different forms of human knowledge is their confirmability by inductive method: an assertion can only be regarded scientifically (empirically) valid if it can be confirmed by inductive method or an inductive inference. As regards a theoretical proposition, it must permit logical reduction to a protocol statement confirmable by an experiment. The basic distinction of Popper's criterion of scientific knowledge from the verification principle consisted in that he regarded *refutability* (or falsifiability) and not confirmability as the main characteristic feature of a scientific statement. Hence Popper's solution of the problem of demarcation between scientific and non-scientific assertion is the direct logical opposite of the neo-positivistic criterion. A system of assertions can only be considered scientific if it is at last capable of being at variance with observation. From this it follows that the verifiability of a theory coincides not with its confirmability but with its refutability. For instance, the existence of God, according to Popper, is asserted in approximately this form:

God is because he is. Since this statement is practically tautological, the degree of its confirmability is very high. Yet it is quite obvious that a statement of this kind is completely immune from refutation and is therefore non-scientific. A scientist is usually not guided by generalised observations, but makes a resolute step and puts forward bold proposals which are subject to subsequent empirical verification. Popper maintains that scientists test new theories not in an attempt to deduce them from a certain imaginary basis, but by creating experimental situations whereby they try to refute or falsify them.

Scientific Activity According to Popper

According to Popper knowledge cannot start from nothing - from a tabula rasa-nor yet from observation. The advance of knowledge consists mainly in the modification of earlier knowledge. For example in archaeology we advance through a chance observation the significance of the discovery will usually depend upon its power to modify our earlier theories. *Refutation* in sciences, according to Popper is a motive force of progress - a refuted hypothesis gives place to another one intended to eliminate or avoid the error. Some conclusion ensuing from an adopted theory or the hypothesis may be refuted-this will cause the scientists to improve and transform the theory or the hypothesis. It may also happen that the very premises of a theory should be resolutely rejected. In any case a scientist himself must always strive to subject his hypothesis to serve criticism as it stimulates continuous progress of science. A refutation in his opinion is a scientists victory since any act of rejection represents the essence of the science of elimination of errors and perpetual progress of knowledge. For example Newton's theory of planetary movements was modified subsequently by Kepler and Einstein. Popper presents a dramatic picture of the evolution of science which consists essentially in a continuous struggle of theories and in the survival of the fittest.

As regards each individual scientific theory it begins, according to Popper with a problem. Then follows a tentative solution, a conjecture, criticism and correction of errors. The tentative solution may prove partly or even completely erroneous. To avoid errors, the scientist must look deeper into the problem and 'comprehend' it. The step that follows a tentative solution consists in discussing and criticising the theory. The critical attitude may be described as the conscious attempt to make our theories or conjectures suffer in our stead in the struggle for the survival of the fittest. It gives us a chance to survive the elimination of an inadequate hypothesis.

Popper dismisses the question of the *source of knowledge*. In this regard he differs from traditional epistemologists or empiricists. Popper's epistemology boils down to *logic of scientific discovery* which is not concerned with such questions. His logic of science is a logic of scientific discovery. Popper's logical notions showed a clear tendency towards historicism in the presentation of scientific progress.

Science is an endless chain of theories that replace one another. Popper effects a radical change in the traditional orientation of the logical analysis of scientific knowledge. For Popper the problem of the criterion of scientificity organically merges with the concept of development of science.

Summary of Popper's Falsification Theory

1) Karl Popper believed that scientific knowledge is provisional.

2) Popper is known for his attempt to refute the classical positivist account of the scientific method by replacing induction with the falsification principle.
3) The first falsification principle proposed by Karl Popper, is a way of demarcating science from non-science. It suggests that for a theory to be considered scientific it must be able to be tested and conceivably proven false.
4) For example, the hypothesis that "all swans are white" can be falsified by observing a black swan.
5) For Popper, science should attempt to disprove a theory than attempt to continually support theoretical hypothesis.
6) Karl popper is prescriptive, and describes what science should do (not how it actually behaves). Popper is a rationalist and contended that the central question in the philosophy of science was distinguishing science from non-science.
7) Karl popper in *the Logic of Scientific Discovery* emerged as a major critic of inductivism, which he saw as an essentially old-fashioned strategy.

Karl Popper and Social Science

As a social scientist Popper advocates democracy and human freedom. The society must protect human freedom from the forces that affect it. In history we find that there had been different political systems like totalitarianism, authoritarianism, capitalism and Marxism. These systems limit human freedom and individual liberty. To a world of such systems, Popper suggests a new form of society known as open society. His whole philosophy of social sciences is based on this.

Popper's social philosophy is not something abstract. It

is something very concrete and it is very relevant to our time. Today it is claimed that there are many democratic countries in the world. But humans have begun to exploit humans under the roof of democracy. Humans have gone to the extent of using the idea of democracy itself to exploit people. Political systems are no more interested in people but rather they are concerned with their own beliefs and interest. At this juncture, open society is a real challenge to us. It demands the present system to reformulate its structure. Democracy will cherish only in an open society. Our political system will gain its meaning if the concept of open society is well understood and well executed. According to Popper an open society is possible only when it is possible for the individual citizens to evaluate critically the consequences of the implementation of government policies. In such a society the individuals have freedom to criticise the administration and its policies.

Popper's Social and Political Thought

Popper's aim and dream is a society which is adapted to problem solving, a kind of society which calls for the bold propounding of trial solutions which are then subjected to criticism and error-elimination. So, his social philosophy is centered on the concept of democracy. When democracy with free institutions is the aim what has to be done is to undo all that is against open society. He felt that history has to be looked at critically and certain systems, that exited in the past have to be critically analysed. As a result of this, Popper comes out with his criticism on totalitarianism, historicism, utopianism and soon. All these systems derived individual rights and liberty and advocated authoritarian society. Popper's *The Poverty of Historicism* is dedicated to the memory of the countless men and women of all creeds or nations or races who fell victims to the fascist and communist beliefs.

Utopianism

Utopianism can be described as a form of rationalism. There are both right and wrong form of rationalism. Utopianism is a wrong form of rationalism. An action is rational when it makes the best use of the available means in order to achieve a certain end. So it is possible that we can judge an action rationally though the end may not be determined rationally. Popper says:

> "However this maybe, we can judge an action rationally and describe it as rational or adequate only relative to some given end. Only if we have an end in mind, and only relative to such an end, can we say that we are acting rationally".[1]

Popper applies this argument to politics. In its application he says that all politics consists of actions and these actions when they pursue some end they will be rational. It is very important to choose our ultimate political action before involving in any rational political action. For example, we must be clear of the kind of state, which we should consider the best before determining the means to realise his state. Popper's conception of Utopianism is that it is to cover any long scale project of social reconstruction. When he says social reconstruction he specifically refers to the view that an ultimate end, which takes the form of a fully worked out plan of an ideal social order should be the guiding factor in rational political action. He is of the view that this holistic conception is disastrously misguided. So he prefers to call it as piecemeal engineering. In this the reform is erected towards the elimination of the most pressing present evils.

Totalitarianism

Totalitarianism refers to a system of government in which there is only one political party, usually demanding that people submit totally to the requirements of the state. Since Popper is insisting on democracy and individual freedom, totalitarianism is an enemy to open society. Popper turns his attention to Plato and makes an analysis of Plato's sociology and his political programme. Plato believed in strict division of the classes (Plato's cardinal virtues). He believed in a philosopher king who is wise enough to rule over the other classes in the society. He even justified slavery. Though Plato did not mean maximum exploitation of the working classes by the upper classes what he intended was the stability of the state-the stability of the whole. So for him such a kind of holism or totalitarianism was amoral.

But according to Popper the idea of totalitarianism is the morality of the closed society. A closed society points to the view of collective selfishness and not even individual selfishness. According to this understanding of collective selfishness good is what is in the interest of the group or the tribe or the state.

This understanding is known as the collectivist, the tribal, the totalitarian theory of morality. As long as the state is strong, its actions are right. It has right even to do violence to its people if that increases its stability or strength. For Plato what is important is the interest of the state. For him everything that is good to the state is just and everything that is not good is unjust. Popper traced the development of modern totalitarianism as exemplified by fascism in Germany and Communism in Russia 'to the spell of Plato' which had been transmitted to the modern west by Hegel and Marx.

Popper's Criticism of Marx

Popper in his attempt to safeguard individual freedom criticizes Marx's *historicism* because in historicism historical prophesies are made. The prophesies are related to Marxian method of social revolutions to achieve the goal. Popper did not agree with Marxian method of revolutions and violence in achieving the end. Social sciences study the behaviour of social wholes. Social wholes refer to groups, nations, classes, societies and civilisations. Social sciences study the social wholes as if they are empirical objects. Popper says that this must be rejected because it does not seem to realise the fact that social wholes are very largely postulates of popular social theories. In fact, they stand for a kind of ideal object. So, social wholes, which are described as naive collectivism have to be replaced by the demand that the individuals in a society and their actions and relations.[2]

Marx believed in recasting social system through social revolution. But revolutionary methods will only make things worse. They will increase unnecessary suffering, lead to more and more violence and destroy freedom. Thus we understand that revolution always destroys the institutional and traditional framework of society. Marx believed always in collectivism and ruling class. But the rationalists oppose historicism and holism which ignore individual freedom. Holism is the view that human social groupings are greater than the sum of their members and shape their destines according to their own independent laws of development. Historicism is the belief that history develops inexorably and necessarily according to certain principles or rules towards a determinable end. Popper feels that both historicism and Holism will lead to authoritarianism. And ultimately we will be led to centralised government control of the individual and attempted imposition of large-scale social planning. Popper is strongly against this view and he promotes the view that any human social groupings are no more than the sum of its individual members.

Popper described Marx as one of the enemies of the open society. He was once a Marxist, but later he became an anti-Marxist. Popper rejected the view that Marxism is scientific. Marxian prophesy of socialism did not come true. Marx misled intelligent people into believing that historical prophecy is the scientific way of approaching social problems.

Popper rejected the Marxism theory of state. According to Marx, "the state is an organ of class *domination,* an organ for the oppression of one class by another; its aim is the creation of an 'order', which legalises and perpetuates this oppression".[3]

But according to Popper even democratic government is a dictatorship of the ruling class over the ruled. Marx believed that social revolution will lead to a better world but in reality it is not so. It is the fact that Marx's theory cannot alter the economic reality by legal reforms. So Popper is of the opinion that this is an extremely poor political programme. What we need is not capitalism, economic historicism or communism no holism but piecemeal social engineering.

Popper's Criticism of Hegel

According to Popper Hegel is the source of all historicism. For Plato the ideas or essences exist prior to the things in flux. But for Hegel ideas or essences are in the things in flux. Hegel believes in the dialectic triad (thesis, anti-thesis and synthesis) and it leads to progress. For Hegel state is an organism. According to Popper, Hegel is totalitarian because his theses are all types of fascism. Hegel's views on nation, state, war, juridical law, power and moral obligation are questioned by Popper. For Popper fascism is a lunatic continuation of Hegel's politics and Hegel produced systematic and influential critique of individualism. Popper considered Hegel as one of the enemies of open society.

Paradox of Democracy and Sovereignty

By democracy what Popper means is the open society. He sees democracy in terms of the presentation of certain kinds of institutions. If it is just the election of governments, then he says it would be the paradox of democracy, because, if majority votes for fascist, which does not believe in free institutions then democracy will come to an end. So Popper's approach is free of this Paradox. There are also other Paradoxes of *tolerance*; any society that extends unlimited tolerance is likely to be destroyed and tolerance with it. It is the indication that a tolerant society must be prepared to suppress the enemies of tolerance. In the paradox of *freedom*, unqualified freedom is self-destructive and also produces its opposite because if there is no restriction then it is impossible to stop the strong from enslaving the weak. This points to us that 'complete freedom' could bring about the end of freedom and therefore proponents of complete freedom are enemies of freedom. Here special reference is made by Popper to the paradox of economic freedom. It is economic freedom that makes possible the unrestrained exploitation of the poor by the rich. Here the power of the state should enforce through its instructions laws to prevent exploitations of the poor by the rich. To be effective the institutions which are like fortresses are to be properly constructed and are to be properly manned.

Paradox of Sovereignty

In any political system, the ultimate question that arises is the question of 'who should rule?' Where should sovereignty lie? Different societies have different power centres. In some the power is diffused. It is not important that we must worry about who should rule but we must think of how to minimise misrule. Popper aims at less damage in the exercise of state power. The general guiding principle for public policy put forward in the open society is; minimise avoidable sufferings, minimise disadvantage to the public, minimum unhappiness and maximise pleasure, maximise the freedom of individuals to live as they wish and move towards freedom.

References

1. Karl Popper, *Conjectures and Refutations: The Growth of Scientific Knowledge*, Routledge, London, 1962, p. 358.

2. Karl Popper, *The Open Society and its Enemies*, Vol. II, Routledge, London, 1945, p. 95.

3. *Ibid.*, p. 118.

CHAPTER VI

SCIENTIFIC REVOLUTION IN PHILOSOPHICAL PERSPECTIVE

Thomas Kuhn's *The Structure of Scientific Revolution,* is a book about the history of science. His book was a landmark event in the *history, philosophy* and *sociology of science.* Kuhn challenged the then prevailing view of progress in science in which scientific progress was viewed as development-by-accumulation of accepted facts and theories. Kuhn argued for an episodic model in which periods of conceptual continuity where there is cumulative progress which Kuhn, referred to as periods of 'normal science', were interrupted by periods of revolutionary science. The discovery of 'anomalies' during revolution in science leads to new *paradigms.* New paradigms then ask new questions of old data, move beyond the mere 'puzzle-solving' of the previous paradigm, change the rules of the game and the "map" directing new research.

Kuhn's approach to the history and philosophy of science focuses on conceptual issues like the practice of *normal science,* influence of historical events, emergence of scientific discoveries, nature of scientific revolutions and progress through scientific revolutions. Kuhn's book argues that evolution of scientific theory does not emerge from the straight forward accumulation of facts, but rather from a set of changing intellectual circumstances and possibilities. Such an approach is largely commensurate with the general historical school of non-linear history.

Kuhn's Paradigm

According to Kuhn, scientific progress is a series of changes in paradigms. The *paradigm shift* according to him is that one paradigm replacing another paradigm. For example, the paradigm of the *geocentric theory* was replaced by another paradigm of *heliocentric theory*. No paradigm is absolute. It is *relative* to the circumstances. The theory that the *sun* revolves round the earth was not disputed by the scientists till Copernicus. The Copernican revolution in planetary motion is, a *paradigm shift*. Later on the Dalton's *atomic theory* was disproved with another theory. The theory of Dalton that *atoms cannot be divided* was rejected with new discoveries in physics. The split of atoms into *electrons, protons* and neutrons was a paradigm shift from the paradigm of indivisibility of atoms held by Dalton's paradigm. One of the aims of science is to find models that will account for as many observations as possible within a coherent framework. Once a paradigm shift has taken place, the textbooks are rewritten. Often the *history of science* too is rewritten, being presented as an inevitable process leading up to the current, established framework of thought. Scientist's puzzle-solving is pursued with great tenacity, because the previous successes of the established paradigm tend to generate great confidence. This process, Kuhn calls *normal science*. In this process anomalies are inevitable, but scientists do not lose faith in establishing alternative paradigms. The conservatives among scientists may not be ready to accept new paradigms. But scientists with exceptional ability and experimental data convince them to accept new paradigms. In time, if the challenging paradigm is solidified and unified, it will replace the old paradigm and a *paradigm shift* will have occurred.

The Function of Dogma

The development of scientific knowledge was given an anti-positivist perspective by Kuhn. In this process he rejected Popper's critical rationalism. Popper ignored the dogmas which persisted in scientific life. These dogmas bolster up the faith of the scientists in their investigations. Kuhn emphasises the function of dogma in scientific investigation. Contrary to Popper who avers that bold refutations and tough competition of theories pave the way for scientific progress, Kuhn sees the starting point of progress in transition from debates and competitive theories to a common viewpoint shared by all specialists.

According to Kuhn, the true creator of science is the scientific community, a group of professionals who decide to adopt a certain scientific achievement or theory as a model and make it a basis for their investigations. No scientific community can start investigating natural phenomena without a definite system of generally recognised notions. Such a system of notions include models of the type, "Heat is kinetic energy of particles making a body" or "All perceptible phenomena are essentially interaction of qualitatively homogeneous atoms in free space", etc. Within the scientific community a model theory is a paradigm whereas the study of nature within the framework of paradigm is "normal science". If there is a paradigm, the solution of concrete scientific problem resembles the solution of puzzles; the scientist has a model of the solution (paradigm), the rules to be followed, and knows that the problem is soluble.

The conditions being set, his success depends on his personal ingenuity. The secret of scientific achievements lies largely in the self-organisation of scientific community. A scientific revolution consists essentially in a change of paradigms. The change of paradigms or turning points in the history of science was witnessed during the life-times of Newton, Lavoisier and Einstein. According to Kuhn, each of these turning points signified that a group of professional scientists had to discard one age-old theory in favour of another incompatible with the former.

Rivalry among Paradigms

In his work, *The Structure of Scientific Revolutions,* Kuhn in the end of the chapter spelled out his views on the nature of scientific progress. Since he considered problem solving to be a central element of science, Kuhn saw that for a new candidate paradigm to be accepted by a scientific community, "First, the new candidate must seem to resolve some outstanding and generally recognized problem that can be met in no other way. Second, the new paradigm must promise to preserve a relatively large part of the concrete problem solving ability that has accrued to science through its predecessors. While the new paradigm is rarely as expensive as the old paradigm in its initial stages, it must nevertheless have significant promise for future problem-solving. As a result, though new paradigms seldom or never possess all the capabilities of their predecessors, they usually preserve a great deal of the most concrete parts of past achievements and they always permit additional concrete problem-solutions besides. Therefore though there seems to be several rival paradigms involved in problem-solving situations the aim is to achieve scientific progress.

Relativism

Kuhn agreed with Michael Polanyi that scientist's *subjective experience* made science a *relativised* discipline. There is no consensus among philosophers about many of the central problems concerned with the philosophy of science including whether science can reveal the truth about *unobservable things* and whether scientific reasoning can be justified at all. In addition to these general questions about science as a whole, philosophers of science consider problems that apply to particular sciences (such as biology or physics). Some philosophers of science also use contemporary results in science to reach conclusions about philosophy itself.

Philosophical thought pertaining to science dates back to the time of Aristotle. In the 20th century it was related to logical positivism. C.S. Peirce and Karl Popper moved on from positivism to establish a modern set of standards for scientific methodology. Thomas Kuhn contributed his paradigm-shift approach to the scientific progress. W.V. Quine gave his *coherentist* approach model to science according to which a theory is validated if it makes sense of observations as part of a coherent whole. Stephen Jay Gould grounded science in *axiomatic* assumptions such as the *uniformity of nature*. Another approach to science involves studying how *knowledge is created* from a sociological perspective. A tradition in contemporary philosophy approaches science from the perspective of a rigorous analysis of human experience. The inter-theoretical approach or *reductionism* in science attempts to study biological phenomena in terms of physics and chemistry. The philosophies of biology, of psychology, and of social sciences explore whether the scientific stitches of human nature can achieve objectivity or are inevitably shaped by *values* and by social relations.

Kuhn's Rejection of Popper's Logical Rules of Scientific Progress

The basic distinction between Popper's and Kuhn's concepts lies in different understanding of the nature of science and progress, Popper has repeatedly emphasised the need to cast of "Psychologism" in the solution of such problems. He was never tired of repeating that his concern was the logical rules of scientific progress rather than the scientist's psychological incentives; yet he could not but admit that the rules of logic followed by scientists in their investigations are something like their professional imperatives. In contrast to Popper, Kuhn contends that such imperatives alone can account for a scientist's selection of one solution instead of another and that his preference cannot be explained on purely *logical* or experimental grounds. In other words, it is only the analysis of *socio-psychological* factors in the development of science that provides a key to the correct understanding of the historical aspects of scientific progress. Popper's science is *impersonal* whereas Kuhn, strives to introduce a *'human element'* into the logical problems of scientific cognition and highlights to sociological and psychological aspects. Popper's logic of science is the logic of scientific discovery, the logic of a radical transformation of the existing system of knowledge. He deviated from logical positivists and emphasised deductive character of the logical structure of knowledge. Popper's concept did not go beyond the limits of empiricism since it proceeded from the direct dependence of a theory on its empirical verification. His logico-methodological system is different from the socio-psychological system of Kuhn.

Thomas Kuhn's Incommensurability

Commensurability is a concept in the philosophy of science whereby scientific theories are commensurable if scientists can discuss them using a shared nomenclature that allows direct comparison of theories to determine which theory is *more valid* or *useful*. On the other hand, theories are incommensurable if they are embedded in starkly contrasting *conceptual framework* whose languages do not overlap sufficiently to permit scientists to directly compare the theories or to cite *empirical evidence* favouring one theory over the other. The problem of incommensurability results in scientists talking past each other, as it were, while comparison of theories is muddled by confusions about terms, contexts and consequences.

Introduction of the Term

In 1962, Thomas Kuhn and Paul Feyerabend both independently introduced the idea of incommensurability to the Philosophy of science. In both cases, the concept came from mathematics; in its original sense, it is defined as the absence of a common unit of measurement of two variables, such as the prediction of the *diagonal* of a *square* from the relationship of its sides. The term commensurability was coined because of a series of problems that both authors found when trying to interpret successive scientific theories. Its implementation is better understood by the antiques of Kuhn and Feyerabend. The *thesis on the accumulation of scientific knowledge* states that the body of *scientific knowledge* has been increasing with the passage of time. Both Kuhn and Feyerabend reject this thesis, in favour of a *model* that sees both *revolutions* and periods of *normalcy* in the history of Science.

Another equally important thesis proposes the existence

of a *neutral language* of comparison which can be used to formulate the empirical consequences of two competing theories. This would allow one to choose the theory with the greatest empirically verified contents of explanatory powers-or the greatest content that is not falsified if the formulation is *Popperian*. 1) The choice between theories presupposes that they can be inter-translated, for example between theory A and its successor B - and in the case of Popper that B can be deduced from A. 2) It is also assumed that the choice is always carried out under the same standards of rationality.

In both cases, the concept of incommensurability makes the viability of the thesis impossible. In the first by showing that certain empirical consequences are lost between successive theories. In the second case, by confirming that it is possible to make a rational choice between theories even when they cannot be translated into a neutral language.

In his book, *The Structure of Scientific Revolution*, Kuhn mentions that the incommensurability is a consequence of the role of *similarity sets* in normal science. Competing paradigms group concepts in different ways, with different similarity relations. This causes fundamental problems in communication between proponents of different paradigms. It is difficult to change such categories in one's mind, because the groups have been learned by means of exemplars instead of definitions. This problem cannot be resolved by using a natural language for communication, according to Kuhn, since the difference occurs prior to the application of language. Kuhn's concept of incommensurability was due to the influence of *Michael Polanyi* on him who held that there can be a logical gap between *belief* systems and who also said that scientist from different schools "think differently, speak different languages, live in a different world"

Criticism on Thomas Kuhn

Karl Popper focuses his evaluation of Kuhn's concept of normal science. Kuhn describes normal science as paradigm-based research in which scientists conduct their research within the theoretical and conceptual provisions of the accepted paradigm. His idea of normal science is very controversial and as such was criticised by many philosophers of science, especially Karl Popper. The basic questions are: What actually does Kuhn mean by normal science? What are the major occupations of scientists during normal scientific research? What are the major criticisms Popper made against Kuhn's normal science? Is Popper right in his assessment of Kuhn's idea of normal science? Popper's fundamental problem is his assessment of Kuhnian normal science in isolation without taking adequate cognizance of its proper context. Nevertheless, Popper's non-dogmatic approach to the scientific investigation could be said to be very necessary for the development of science in general.

What is normal science according to Kuhn?

Normal science focuses on the accepted beliefs of a given scientific community which forms the paradigm for scientific research. Kuhn conceives it as the normal condition of scientific research in which scientists are trained to engage in. It is the usual activity of scientists and such activities are based on past scientific achievements which are models for scientific investigation. Thus it is obvious from Kuhn's stipulation that it is past scientific achievements that guide the conduct of normal science. Kuhn cites Aristotle's physics, Newton's principles, Lavoisier's chemistry etc; as vivid examples of past scientific achievements. Such past scientific achievements are models for scientific research, and as such scientists conduct their research within their theoretical and conceptual provisions. They are the accepted examples of actual scientific practice, which guide scientists in the conduct of scientific research during the period of normal science.

Normal science faces problems when new puzzles or anomalies arise in scientific research. A new crisis situation arises which requires new paradigms in scientific research. Therefore new crisis situations in scientific research forces the scientists to shift to new paradigms in science.

Concept of Paradigm

Stephen Toulmin defined paradigm as "the set of common beliefs and agreements shared between scientists about how problems should be understood and addressed. He argued in his *Human understanding* (1972) that a more realistic picture of science than that presented in *the Structure of Scientific Revolution* would admit the fact that revisions in science take place much more frequently, and are much less dramatic than can be explained by the model of revolution/normal science. In Toulmin's view, such revisions occur quite often during periods of what Kuhn would call "normal science".

Incommensurability of Paradigm

Carl R. Kordig's criticism of the Kuhnian position was that the incommensurability thesis was too radical and that this made it impossible to explain the confrontation of scientific theories that actually occurs. According to Kordig, it is in fact possible to admit the existence of revolutions and paradigm shifts in science while still recognising that theories belonging to different paradigms can he compared and confronted on the plane of observation. Those who accepted the incommensurability thesis do so because they admit the discontinuity of paradigms, but because they attribute a radical change in meanings to such shifts.

Kordig maintains that there is a common observational plane. For example, when Kepler and Tycho Brahe are trying to explain the relative variation of the distance of the sun from the horizon and sunrise, both see the same thing (the same configuration is focused on the retina of each individual). This is just one example of the fact that rival scientific theories share some observations, and therefore some meanings". Kordig suggests that with this approach, he is not reintroducing the distinction between observation and theory in which the former is assigned a privileged and neutral status, but that it is possible to affirm more simply the fact that, even if no sharp distinction exists between theory and observation, this does not imply there are no comprehensible differences at the two extremes of this polarity.

At a secondary level, for Kordig there is a common plane of inter-paradigmatic standards of shared norms that permit the effective confrontation of rival theories.

Summary of Kuhn's The Structure of Scientific Revolution

In "The Structure of Scientific Revolution", Thomas Kuhn presents a revolutionary approach to how science functions and progresses. Against the normal perception of science as a linear accommodation of knowledge, Kuhn attempts to view science as progressing in leaps from one "paradigm" to the next.

Kuhn is revolutionary in the philosophy of science since he views scientific practice as something conducted by community rather than a set of individuals. As a community the scientific world is *sociological* matter, especially in terms of having norms and common held beliefs which functions within it and regulate it. Kuhn argues for example that scientific education is in fact the socialisation or indoctrination of the young researcher into the conventional manner in which science is practised. This is what Kuhn famously calls "paradigm" the unspoken basic assumption which makes the world view of a scientific community and allows it to function.

In *"The Structure of Scientific Revolution"* Kuhn describes the history of science as a progression from one paradigm to the next. When a certain paradigm is enough to account for the world as it is perceived, "normal science" can function, elaborating knowledge within the paradigm. But when new paradigm enters a crisis in meeting phenomenon, it cannot account for internal contradiction, the search for new paradigm is on.

What happens eventually according to Kuhn is that the paradigmatic crisis leads to scientific revolution which marks a shift, even rupture, from the pre-existing paradigm. This means that all prior knowledge has to be reintegrated into the concept and structures of the new paradigm. When this is complete science can once again function as "normal science" until the next paradigm crisis and scientific revolution. Changing paradigms is similar to a religious conversion, which also draws heavy contention from conservative process. Kuhn's "The Structure of Scientific Revolution" is considered to mark the postmodern turn in the philosophy of science making human knowledge a relative field of belief as much as it is of objective knowledge.

PART II

CHAPTER VII

PHILOSOPHY OF MATHEMATICS

History of Mathematics

The history of mathematics deals with the origin of discoveries in mathematics and the mathematical methods and notation of the past. From 3000 BCE, the *Mesopotamian* states of *Sumer, Akkad* and *Assyria* followed closely by Ancient *Egypt* and the *Levantine* state of *Ebla* began using *arithmetic, algebra* and *geometry* for purposes of taxation commerce, trade and also in the patterns in nature, the field of astronomy and to record time and formulate calendars. The earliest mathematical texts available are from *Mesopotamia* and *Egypt*. The Pythagorean Theorem seems to be the most ancient and widespread mathematical development after basic arithmetic and geometry. The Greek mathematics greatly refined the methods through the introduction of deductive reasoning and the mathematical rigor in proofs. Though the Greeks made no contribution to theoretical mathematics, the ancient Romans used applied mathematics in *surveying, structural engineering, mechanical engineering,* bookkeeping, creation of lunar and solar calendars, and even *arts* and *crafts*. Chinese mathematics made early contributions including a *place value system* and the first use of negative numbers. The *Hindu-Arabic* numeral system and the rules for the use of its operations in use throughout the world today evolved over the course of the first millennium CE in India and were transmitted to the western world, via. Islamic mathematics through the work of Muhammad bin Musa-al-Khwarizmi. Islamic mathematics in turn developed and expanded the mathematics known to these civilisations. Contemporaneous with but independent of these traditions were the mathematics developed by the *Maya civilisation* of *Mexico* and *Central America* where the concept of zero was given a standard symbol in *Maya numerals.*

Many Greek and Arabic text on mathematics were translated into *Latin* from twelfth century onward, leading to further development of mathematics in Medieval Europe. Beginning in Renaissance Italy in the fifteenth century new discoveries in science were made. This includes the groundbreaking works of both Leibniz and Isaac Newton. Leibniz published his work on infinitesimal *calculus* followed by Newton in seventeenth century. René Descartes synthesized arithmetics and Geometry through his analytical geometry Even to-day the graphical representation of x and y co-ordinates are called *Cartesian* co-ordinates named after Descartes.

Philosophy of Mathematics

Philosophising mathematics is traceable to the Greek period. The mathematical object such as Numbers are related to "forms" by Plato which is rejected by Aristotle. The problems in the Philosophy of mathematics include :

1. The content of mathematics and its evolution.

2. The central principles of mathematics.
3. The source of the reality of mathematics.
4. The methods of mathematics.
5. The regions of validity of mathematics.[1]

Both Arithmetic and Geometry are the foundations of mathematics. Apart from Arithmetics and Geometry there are different approaches to mathematics: 1) Logicism (Frege, Russell and set theory); 2) Formalism (Hilbert, Gödel); 3) Intuitionism (Brouwer); 4) Predicativism (Russell); and 5) Realism and Nominalism (Gödel, Neo-Fregeans and Quine).[2]

Platonism in Mathematics

Platonism in the philosophy of mathematics has two main claims. The first is ontological: mathematics is about real objects, which must be regarded as genuinely existing, even though (in the metaphor) they do not exist 'in This world'. For Plato the objects of mathematics are not 'perceptible objects', but 'intelligible objects'. The main claim is that they do exist, but are not objects of sense-perception. The second claim is epistemological: we do know quite a lot about these objects, for mathematical knowledge genuinely is *knowledge*, but this knowledge is not based upon perception. It is a priori knowledge. However in Platonism there is no entailment between ontology and epistemology.

Aristotle

Aristotle rejects Platonic account of mathematics. For him Plato was wrong to 'separate' the objects of knowledge from the ordinary objects of this world. He agrees with Plato that there are things which can be called "forms" and that knowledge is always knowledge of such forms, but he claims against Plato that these forms have no existence apart from their instances in this world. For example, there is a form of man, and there is a form of circle, but these forms exist only *in* actual men and actual circular objects (such as the top of a round table). He firmly denies the Platonic idea that there are "two worlds", one containing perceptible objects and the other imperceptible but intelligible objects. There is only one world, and it is that world that mathematics is about. The truths of mathematics are truths about perfectly ordinary objects, but truths at a high level of generality. On the topic of epistemology Aristotle similarly claims that our knowledge of such truths is again perfectly ordinary empirical knowledge based upon perception. He supposes that if mathematics need not be understood as concerned with a special and 'separate' kind of object, then equally our mathematical knowledge need not be credited to a special and rather peculiar faculty for 'a priori' knowledge. So both Platonic ontology and the Platonic epistemology are rejected by Aristotle. The Platonist thinks that all the numbers have an actual existence, in separation from the perceptible things of this world. Aristotle assumes that in this case the Platonist must accept that there is such a thing as the number of all the numbers. If so, then this number must be an infinite number. But Aristotle thinks that it is impossible for there to be such a thing as an infinite number a) because, since a number can always be reached by counting, this would mean that one could count to infinity, and b) because every number must be either odd or even but an infinite number would not be either. The problem of infinity cannot be explained satisfactorily by both Plato and Aristotle. In opposition to Plato, Aristotle is aiming for an empirical theory of mathematics, which does not accept the real existence of any objects that are not empirically available. But the empirical possibility of infinite number is not explained by Aristotle. If infinity cannot be explained by Aristotle one has to accept Platonism.[3]

Aristotle and Problems of Infinity

Aristotle says that all infinity is always potential, which apparently implies that it cannot even be actual. An infinite totality could exist only as the result of an infinite process being completed. He believes that an infinite process cannot be completed. So there can never be a completed infinite totality. No doubt most processes will stop at some time, though they may be said to be potentially infinite been continued further. Aristotle applies this general view to the supposed infinite divisibility of a geometrical object, such as process of dividing a finite line into parts. To cite Zeno's well known example, one may take half of a line, and then half of what remains, and then half of what still remains, and so on forever. But Aristotle holds that these parts, and the points that would divide them from one another, do not *actually* exist until the divisions are actually made. This is because, if they do exist, then one who moves over a finite distance must have completed an infinite series of smaller movements, each half as long as its predecessor, which he regards as impossible. So, his idea is that one who simply moves in a continuous way over a certain distance does not count as' actualising' any point on that distance. The general idea is that to 'actualise' a point one must *do* something, at or to that point, which singles it out from all neighbouring points. And the thought is that no infinite series of such doings could be completed in a finite time. Consequently a finite line never will contain infinitely many actual points (or actual parts, but we can still say that its divisibility is 'potentially infinite', on the ground that, however many divisions have been made so far, another is always possible).[4]

From Aristotle to Kant

From Aristotle to Descartes Philosophers paid little attention to the nature of Mathematics. It was generally accepted that the truths of mathematics are eternal and unchanging truths, and deserve to be called necessary truths. Very few questioned about their ontological status (the numbers, geometrical figures and so on). The Philosophical question is: Do numbers (universals) exist? If so, do they exist outside the mind or simply as mental entities. Are numbers corporate or incorporate? And do they exist *in* the things that are perceptible by the senses, or are they separate from such things? The realist says that universals do exist outside human minds, and independently of all human thought. Plato and Aristotle were both realists in this sense, though Plato held that universals existed separately from perceptible things. In modern mathematics there are realists of the Platonic type, e.g. *Frege* and *Gödel*. The conceptualist says that universals exist only in the mind. According to the nominalist universals do not exist.

Descartes

Descartes is regarded as the founder of modern Philosophy. His quest for certainty began with the thought that in mathematics we do find certainty. All our beliefs about the physical world are all based upon the senses. The senses may sometimes deceive us. One can doubt whether there is a physical world at all. Descartes took it to follow that if mathematics enjoys a certainty that our physical beliefs lack, then the truths of mathematics cannot be truths about physical world. They must instead be truths about our ideas, or perhaps about some feature of the mind of God that determines those ideas of ours. In Descartes's view mathematics is a theory of certain mental objects called 'ideas', which can only exist in minds. In Plato's view mathematics is a theory of certain abstract objects, which exist independently of any kind of thought or minds. But the main negative thrust is in each case similar: these objects do not owe their existence to anything perceptible, neither to perceptible objects (Plato), nor to perceptible ideas (Descartes). In epistemology both Descartes and Plato hold that our knowledge of mathematical object is wholly a *priori.* For both mathematical knowledge is certain and indubitable.[5]

Though Locke, Berkeley and Hume were empiricists, they agreed with rationalist Descartes' view that mathematical truth is an idea. However they did not agree with Descartes' innate ideas. During the time of Berkeley and Hume mathematics included the "infinitesimal calculus" of Newton and Leibnitz. The "infinitesimal quantities" of calculus were beyond their empirical understanding. They began to view that mathematics had gone too far and over reached itself, with the result that it was now a source of impossible contradictions.

Kant believed that the truths of mathematics are both known a priori and synthetic, and his problem was to explain how such knowledge might be possible. In his *Critique of Pure Reason,* he explains the two notions, and sets out his two claims that both apply to mathematical truths. Arithmetics and Geometry can be known a priori and there is role of intuition in mathematics for Kant. For him "7+5=12" is both synthetic and a priori. If we look closely, we find that the concept of the sum of 7 and 5 contains nothing save the union of the two numbers into one and in this no thought is being taken as to what the single number may be which combines both. His idea is that to this single number we must actually do the sum - e.g. by counting on our fingers - and this takes us beyond mere analysis of concepts. The concept of 12 cannot actually be a *part* of the concept of 7 +5, or vice versa, since it is possible to possess either concept without possessing the other. It is obviously possible to have the concept of 12, but not of 7+5. It is also possible to have the concept of 7+5, but not that of 12. For him many propositions of ordinary geometry (Euclidean) are not analytic: no analysis of the concepts involved will tell us that they must be true of the space that we perceive. But such propositions are not known a priori. However for Kant both arithmetic and geometry are synthetic and known a priori. Space and time, though condition our empirical experience involving our sense organs, cannot be known. So for Kant space and Time are forms of intuition. In his *Transcendental Aesthetic,* Kant claimed that space is what he calls 'a priori intuition'. Spatial and temporal concepts can be 'constructed in intuition'. Geometry is concerned with space and arithmetics is concerned with time.

Structuralism

In mathematics we do not have objects with an 'internal' composition arranged in structures, we have only structures. The objects of mathematics, that is, the entities which our mathematical constants and quantifiers denote, are structureless points or positions in structures. As positions in structures, they have no identity or features outside of a structure.[6] The structuralist holds that the subject matter of, say, arithmetic, is a single abstract structure, the natural number structure. Natural numbers are the places of this structure. Structures are prior to places in the same sense that any organisation is prior to the offices that constitute it. The natural-number structure is prior to "6" just as "baseball defence" is prior to "shortstop" or U.S. Government is prior to "vice president". Two interrelated groups of Ontological questions arise, one concerning structures themselves and the other concerning places in structures. There are several ontological views concerning structures. One can be a Platonist, an Aristotelian, a nominalist and soon. For example the natural-number structure, the real-number structure, the set-theoretic hierarchy, and so on. These structures exist whether or not there are systems of objects structured.[7] Structuralism maintains that mathematical objects do not possess any intrinsic properties but are defined by their external relations in a system. For instance, structuralism holds that number 1 is exhaustively defined by being the successor of 0 in the structure of the theory of *natural numbers*. By generalisation of this example, any natural number is defined by its respective place in this structure of the *number line*. Other examples of mathematical objects might include *lines* and *planes* in *geometry*, or elements and operations in abstract algebra.

Structuralism is an *epistemologically realistic view* in that it holds that mathematical statements have an objective *truth value*. However, its central claim only relates to what *kind* of entity a mathematical object is, not to what kind of existence mathematical objects have would clearly be dependent on that of the structure in which they are embedded; different sub-varieties of structuralism make different ontological claims in this regard.

Structuralism in philosophy of mathematics is particularly associated with Paul Benacerraf, Geoffrey Hellman, Michael Resnik, Stewart Shapiro and James Franklin.

Mathematical Logic

Mathematical logic is the study of formal logic within mathematics. Major sub areas include model theory, proof theory, set theory and recursion theory. Research in mathematical logic commonly addresses the mathematical properties of formal systems of logic such as their expressive or deductive power. However, it can also include uses of logic to characterise correct mathematical reasoning or to establish foundations of mathematics. Since its inception, mathematical logic has both contributed to, and has been motivated by, the study of foundations of mathematics. The study began in the late nineteenth century with the development of axiomatic frameworks for geometry, arithmetic and analysis. In the early twentieth century it was shaped by David Hilbert's program to prove the consistency of foundational theories. Work in set theory showed that almost all ordinary mathematics can be formalised in terms of sets, although there are some theorems that cannot be proven in common axiom systems for set theory. Computability theory, also known as *recursion theory* is a branch of *mathematical logic* computer science, and the theory of computation. Basic questions addressed by computability theory include:

a) What does it mean for a function on the *natural numbers* to be computable?

b) How can non-computable functions be classified into a hierarchy based on their level of non-computability.

At its core, mathematical logic deals with mathematical concepts expressed using formal *logical systems*. These systems, though they differ in many details, share the common property of considering only expression in a fixed formal language. The systems of *propositional logic* and first order logic are the most widely studied today because of their applicability to *foundations of mathematics* and because of their desirable proof-theoretic properties. Stronger classical logics such as second-order logic or *infinity logic* are also studied, along with non-classical logics such as *intuitionistic logic*. According to Bertrand Russell, "all mathematical constants are logical constants...... Thus some of the premises of mathematics, e.g. the principle of syllogism, "if p implies q and q implies r, then p implies r" will belong to mathematics, while others such as "implication is a relation" will belong to logic but not to mathematics."[8]

The Frege-Russell account of logicism is criticized for their problems in distinguishing empirical and non-empirical concepts. Logicism is also criticized for not adequately explaining geometry and mathematical infinity.

Intuitionism in Mathematics

Mathematical intuition or logical intuition is a series of instinctive foresight, knowhow, and savviness often associated with the ability to perceive logical truth- and the ability to solve mathematical challenges efficiently. Humans apply logical intuition in proving mathematical theorems, validating logical arguments, developing algorithms and heuristics, and in related contexts where mathematical challenges are involved. The ability to recognize logical or mathematical truth and identify viable methods may vary from person to person, and may even be result of knowledge and experience, which are subject to cultivation. The ability may not be realisable in a computer program by means other than genetic programming or evolutionary programming. Gödel says that mathematical intuition need not be conceived of as a faculty giving an immediate knowledge of the object concerned.[9] Kant expresses puzzlement about how intuition can be a priori. In the *Prolegomena,* after introducing the notion of pure intuition, he writes: An intuition is such a representation as would immediately depend on the presence of the object. Hence it seems impossible to intuit spontaneously *a prior* because intuition would in that event have to take place without either a former or a present object to refer to, and in consequence could not be an intuition. But how can the intuition of an object precede the object itself?[10] Kant does not explicitly express a view about intuition of *mathematical* objects. He claims that a priori intuition contains only the form of our sensibility.

Are natural numbers objects of intuition? Intuition gives objects which form a model of arithmetic, and this model is as good as any, both for the foundations of arithmetic and for applications. But it may not be right to say that the natural numbers are objects of intuition, since intuition does not give a unique sequence to be 'the' natural numbers and the concept of number does not rule out as the 'intended model' objects that are not object of intuition.[11]

Various concepts in mathematics are acquired by means of a complex interaction between a human being and the world over a period of time. To have a concept is to have the ability to acquire certain beliefs, in particular, in the cases we are concerned, the ability to acquire perceptual beliefs about particular things of the kind concerned on appropriate occasions. It has been theorised that a complex mental structure is the source of the ability to acquire these perceptual beliefs - thus, one perceives a triangle, physical object, or set-detector is stimulated. For example, three sidedness is, in a sense 'built into' the triangle detector in the form of mechanisms stimulating eye movements from one corner to another just as three-angledness is built in the form of the detector's three distinct cell assemblies for the corners themselves. Crudely put, then, the very form of one's triangle-detector guarantees that one believe any triangle to be three sided. This is, in effect, a general belief about triangles. A child of 3 is perfectly capable of perceiving physical objects and thus has some of these general beliefs, but lacks the linguistic equipment to express them like adults. The adults have intuitive beliefs about the mathematical objects such as geometrical figures, numbers and sets.[12]

Intuitionism in mathematics is criticised on the ground that intuitionistic mathematics has intimate connection with intuitionist philosophy. There are interrelations between *formalism* and *intuitionism*. Hilbert argues that infinity can have three philosophical positions: finitism, transfinitism, and methodological transfinitism. Intuitionism is a moderate finitism. Intuitionism is also related to the doctrine of potential infinity. Intuition faces difficulty in explaining the logical status of applied mathematics. The formalist's account of the subject matter of mathematics is not analytic, but synthetic whereas the intuitionist's account is synthetic but not non-empirical. For the intuitionist every mathematical statement is justifiable only if, it is self-evident. But the scientists can validate a statement only if it is inter-subjectively corroborated.[13]

Formalism in mathematics

Formalism In mathematics, a school of thought introduced by the twentieth century German mathematician David Hilbert, which holds that all mathematics can be reduced to rules for manipulating formulas without any referent to the meanings of the formulas. Formalists contend that it is the mathematical symbols themselves, and not any meaning that might be ascribed to them, that are the basic objects of mathematical thought. In the philosophy of mathematics, formalism is the view that holds that statements of mathematics and logic can be considered to be statements about the consequences of the manipulation of strings using established manipulation rules. A central idea of formalism "is that mathematics is not a body of propositions representing an abstract sector of reality, but is much more akin to game, bringing with it no more commitment to an *ontology* of objects or properties than *ludo* or *chess*.

According to formalism, the truths expressed in logic and mathematics are not about numbers, sets or triangles or any other coextensive subject matter - in fact, they are not "about" anything at all. Rather mathematical statements are *syntactic* forms whose shapes and locations have no meaning unless they are given an interpretation (or semantics). In contrast to *logicism* or *intuitionism* formalism's contours are less defined due to broad approaches that can be categorised as formalist.

Along with logicism and intuitionism, formalism is one of the main theories in the philosophy of mathematics that developed in the late nineteenth century and early twentieth century.

Kurt Gödel indicated one of the weak points of formalism by addressing the question of consistency in axiomatic systems. Bertrand Russell has argued that formalism fails to explain what is meant by the linguistic application of numbers in statements such as "there are three men in the room". Formalist philosophers of mathematics are aware of the idealised, non-empirical character of certain mathematical concepts in particular the notion of actual infinities. Yet they do not seem to realise that the disconnection of mathematics from perception - the introduction of non-empirical concept - takes place not at the transition from the elementary arithmetic to the amplified, but at the very outset of any development of the elementary. The concept of natural number itself is non-empirical. The formalist is also criticised for his views on applied mathematics, concept of actual infinity and his conception of logic.[14]

Nominalism in Mathematics

Traditionally nominalism is the doctrine that there are no abstract objects. It is called "nominalism" because it starts from the observation that there are in the language words which appear to be names (nomina) of such objects, but it claims that these words do not in fact name anything. The *usual* version of the theory is that sentences containing such words are very often true, because these words are not really names at all, but have another role. The sentences containing them are short for what could be expressed more long-windedly without using the apparent names. For example one may say that the abstract nouns are introduced 'for brevity' without supposing that the word 'brevity' is here functioning as the name of an abstract object. For (in most contexts) the phrase 'for brevity' is merely an idiomatic variant on 'in order to be brief' and this latter does not even look as if it refers to an abstract object named 'brevity'. A theory of this kind may be called 'reductive nominalism', for it promises to show statements which apparently refer to abstract objects may be 'reduced' (without loss of meaning) to other statements which avoid this appearance.[15]

Nominalism maintains that mathematical objects, relations and structures do not exist as abstract objects (They are neither located in space-time nor do they have causal powers). In the latter case, some suitable concrete replacement for mathematical object is provided. Broadly speaking there are two forms of mathematical nominalism: those views that require the reformulation of mathematical theories and those views that do not reformulate mathematical or scientific theories. Both the forms of nominalism have to be examined to address the central problems in the philosophy of mathematics: Epistemology, ontology, the application of mathematics and the use of a uniform semantics. Nominalism concurs with Godel's version of realism according to which mathematical objects exist independent of mind.

Most nominalists have held that only physical particulars in space and time are real, and that universals exist subsequent to particular things. However some versions of nominalism hold that some particulars are abstract entities (e.g. numbers), while others are concrete entities –entities that do exist in space and time (e.g., pillars, snakes, bananas). Nominalism is primarily a position on the *problem of universals,* which dates back at least to Plato and is opposed to *realist* philosophies such as *Platonic realism,* which assert that universals do exist over and above particulars, and to the *hylomorphic* substance theory of Aristotle, which asserts that universals are *immanently real* within them. However the name 'nominalism' emerged from debates in medieval philosophy with *Roscellinus*. The term 'nominalism' stems from the Latin *nomen,* "name". In *philosophy of law,* nominalism finds its application in what is called *constitutional nominalism*.

Indian Mathematics

Indian mathematics emerged in the Indian subcontinent from 1200 BCE until the end of the eighteenth century. In the classical period of Indian mathematics important contributions were made by scholars like *Aryabhatta, Brahmagupta, Bhaskara* II, and *Varahamihira*. The *decimal number system* in use today was first recorded in Indian mathematics. Indian mathematics made early contributions to the study of the concept of *Zero* as a number, *negative numbers, arithmetic,* and *algebra*. In addition, *trigonometry* was further advanced in India, and, in particular the modern definitions of *sine* and *cosine* were developed there. These mathematical concepts were transmitted to the Middle East, China and Europe and led to further developments that now form the foundations of many areas of mathematics.

Ancient and medieval Indian mathematical works, all composed in *Sanskrit,* usually consisted of a section of *sutras* in which a set of rules or problems were stated with great economy in verse in order to aid memorization by a second section consisting of a prose commentary that explained the problems in more detail and provided justification for the solution. In the prose section, the form (and therefore its memorisation) was not considered so important as the ideas involved. All mathematical works were orally transmitted until approximately 500 BCE; thereafter, they were transmitted both orally and in manuscript form. The oldest extant mathematical *document* produced on the Indian subcontinent is the birch bark *Bakhshali manuscript* discovered in 1881 in the village of *Bakhshali,* near Peshawar (now in Pakistan) and is likely from the seventh century CE.

A later landmark in Indian mathematics was the development of the *serious* expansion for *trigonometric functions* (sine, cosine, and arc tangent) by mathematicians of *Kerala School* in the fifteenth century CE. Their remarkable work, completed two centuries before the invention of *calculus* in Europe, provide what is now considered the first example of a *power series* (apart from geometric series). However, they did not formulate a systematic theory of *differentiation* and *integration* nor is their results bring transmitted outside Kerala.

Mathematics in Indus Valley Civilisation

Excavation at Harappa, Mohenjo-daro and other sites of the Indus valley civilisation have uncovered evidence of the use of *practical mathematics*. The people of the Indus valley civilization manufactured bricks whose dimensions were in the proportion 4:2:1, considered favourable for the stability of a brick structure. They mass produced weights in regular *geometrical* shapes, which included *hexahedra, barrels, cones* and *cylinders,* thereby demonstrating knowledge of basic *geometry*.

The inhabitants of Indus civilisation also tried to standardize measurements of length to a high degree of accuracy. They designed a ruler-*the Mohenjo-daro ruler*-whose unit of length (approximately 1.32 inches or 3.4 centimetres) was divided into the equal parts. Bricks manufactured in ancient Mohenjo-daro often had dimensions that were integral multiples of this unit of length.

Hollow cylindrical objects made of shell and formed at Lothal (2200 BCE) and Dholavira are demonstrated to have the ability to measure angles in a plane, as well as to determine the positions of stars for navigation.

Vedic Period

The religious texts of the *Vedic period* provide evidence for the use of *large numbers*. By the time of the *Yajurveda samhita* (1200-900 BCE) numbers as high as 10^{12} were being included in the texts. For example, the *mantra* at the end of *annahoma* (food oblation rite) performed during the *ashvamedha,* and uttered just before, during and just after sunrise, invokes, powers of ten from a hundred to trillion.

Hail to *sata* ("hundred", 10^2), hail

to *sahasra* ("thousand", 10^3), hail

to *ayuta* ("ten thousand", 10^4), hail

to niyuta ("hundred thousand", 10^5), hail

to prayuta ("million", 10^6), hail to

arbude ("ten million", 10^7), hail to

nyarbude ("hundred million", 10^8), hail

to *samudra* ("billion", 10^9, literally ocean),

hail to *madhya* ("ten billion", 10^{10}, literally

middle), hail to *anta* ("hundred billion", 10^{11}, lit., "end"), hail to *parardha*

("one trillion", 10^{12} lit, beyond parts)

hail to the *usas* (dawn), hail to the *vyusti* (twilight), hail to *udyat* (the one which rising), hail

udita (to the one which has just risen), hail to *svarga* (the heaven)

hail to *martya* (the world), hail to all.

Vyakarna

An important landmark of the Vedic period was the work of *Sanskrit grammarian, Panini* (520-460 BCE). His grammar includes early use of *Boolean logic,* of the null operator, and of context free grammars, and includes precursor of the Backus-Naur form (used in the description programming language).

Among the scholars of the post-Vedic period who contributed to mathematics, the most notable is *Pingala* (300-200 BCE), a music theorist who authored the *Chhandas Shastra,* a Sanskrit treatise on *prosody.*

Katyayana

Katyayana (third century BCE) is notable for being the last of the Vedic mathematicians. He wrote the *Katyayana Shulba sutra,* which presented much *geometry,* including the general *Pythagorean theorem,* and a computation of the *square root of* 2 correct to five decimal places.

Jain Mathematics

Jain mathematics is important historically as a crucial link between the mathematics of the vedic period and that of the 'classical period'. A significant historical contribution of Jain mathematician lay in their freeing Indian mathematics from its religions and ritualistic constraints. In particular their fascination with the enumeration of very large numbers and infinites led them to classify numbers into three classes: enumerables, innumerable, and *infinite.* Not content with a simple notion of infinity, their texts define five different types of infinity: the infinite in one direction, the infinite in two directions, the infinite in area, the infinite everywhere, and the infinite perpetually. In addition Jain mathematicians devised notations for simple powers (and exponents) of numbers like squares and cubes, which enabled them to define simple algebraic equations (*bijaganita samikaran*). Jain mathematicians were apparently also the first to use the word *Shunya* (literally void in Sanskrit) to refer to Zero. More than a millennium later their appellation became the English word 'zero' after a tortuous journey of translations and transliterations from India to Europe.

In addition to *Surya Prajnapti,* important Jain works on mathematics included the *Sthananga Sutra* (300 BCE - 200 CE); the *Anuyogadwara Sutra* (200 BCE - 100 CE) which includes the earliest known description of factorials in Indian mathematics; and the *Shatkhandagama* (second century CE, Important Jain mathematicians included Bhadrabahu (298 BCE), the author of two astronomical works, the *Bhadrabahu-Samhita* and a commentary on the *Surya Prajnapti*; Yativrishabha Acharya (176 BCE) who authored a mathematical text called *Tiloya Panatti*; and *Umasvati* (150 BCE), who although better known for his influential writing on Jain philosophy and metaphysics, composed a mathematical work called *Tattwarthadhigama-Sutra Bhashya*.

Mathematics of Ancient Tamils

The huge temple structures and Kallanai (the dam constructed by Karikala Cholan near Trichy) across the river Kaveri in Tamil Nadu reveal that the ancient Tamils had knowledge of mathematics, civil engineering and design, though many sources of the treasure have been lost. The dam built by the Chola king is nearly 2000 years old. *Yerambam* (ஏரம்பம்) was an ancient mathematical treatise in the Tamil language. It was among the few ancient Tamil works on mathematics such as the work of *kanakkadhigaram* (கணக்கதிகாரம்) and the manuscripts of *Kilvaai* and *Kulimaatru*.[16] Yerambam includes several other works such as *kilaralaabam, Adhisaram Kalambagam, Thirubuvana Thilagham, KanithaRathinam,* and Sirukanakku. In addition to these, there were two other works for which the name of the author is known: *Kanakku Nool* by *Kakkai Paadiniyar* and *Kanakkadhigaram* by *Kaarinayanar*. *Kaarinaayanar* cites *Yerambam* and the six other works in the ancient corpus as the sources of his work *Kanakkadhigaram*. According to *Devaneya Pavanar*, the work is completely lost to modern times.[17]

References

1. James B. Shaw, *Lectures on The Philosophy of Mathematics*, Cosmo Publications, New Delhi, 2008, p. 6.

2. David Bostock, *Philosophy of Mathematics-An Introduction,* Wiley-Blackwell, 2009, pp. VI & VIII.

3. *Ibid.,* p. 16.

4. *Ibid.,* pp. 25-26.

5. *Ibid.,* pp. 35, 37.

6. Michell D. Resnik, 'Mathematics as a Science of Patterns: Ontology and Reference', *Nous,* 15 (1981), 530.

7. Stewart Shapiro, *Philosophy of Mathematics: Structure and Ontology,* Oxford University Press, 1997, p. 9.

8. Bertrand Russell, *The Principles of Mathematics,* George Allen & Union, London, 1985, pp. 8-9.

9. W.D. Hart, *The Philosophy of Mathematics,* Oxford University Press, London, 2005, pp. 98-99.

10. *Ibid.,* p. 99.

11. *Ibid.,* p. 111.

12. *Ibid.,* p. 132.

13. Stephan Korner, *The Philosophy of Mathematics,* Dover Publications Inc, New York, 2000, pp. 135ff.

14. *Ibid.,* p. 106.

15. David Bostock, *Philosophy of Mathematics- An Introduction,* Wiley-Blackwell, U.K., 2009, p. 282.

16. A.K. Selvaganapathi (6th March 2011), "தமிழின் கண்கள்" (The eyes of Tamil), Tamilmani, Retrieved 18 March 2011.

17. Nandivarman, Pudhuvai (n.d), தமிழர்நாடும்தனிப்பண்பாடும் (The land of the Tamils and their unique culture), Chennai, Arjuna Padippagam.

CHAPTER VIII

THE STRUCTURE OF UNIVERSE

Structure of Matter

What is the world surrounding us made of? The first answers to this question which have reached us originated in Ancient Greece more than 25 centuries ago. Thales asserted that everything consists of water; Anaximander said that the world is made of air and Heraclitus opined that everything consists of fire. The incongruity of such explanations forced later Greek philosophers to increase the number of fundamental principles (elements). Empedocles asserted that there are four elements: earth, water, air and fire. According to Aristotle all bodies consist of one and the same substance, but this substance can assume different qualities. There are four immaterial elements: cold, hot, moist and dry. Combining in pairs and being imparted to a substance, Aristotle's elements form the elements of Empedocles. Thus, a dry and cold substance yields earth; dry and hot, fire; moist and cold, water and finally, moist and hot, air. However in view of the difficulty involved in answering many questions, ancient philosophies introduced the concept of "god" who cooked various, elements together. Till eighteenth century Aristotle's views were not challenged. In the seventeenth century it became obvious to many people that the number of basic substances-elements-is incomparably greater than four. In 1661 CE, in England, Robert Boyle (1627-1691) published the book. *The Skeptical Chemist* in which he gave a completely new definition of element which is consistent with the modern definition of the concept of an element. French man Lavoisier (1743-1794) who was regarded as the founder of chemistry distinguished heat-producing substance from light-producing substances. In the first half of eighteenth century there were 15 known elements and their number rose to 35 by the end of the century. By the middle of nineteenth century, more than 50 substances were described in chemical hand book. Russian chemist *Mendeleev* (1834-1907) provided the periodic law and showed how one must look for the elements which had not yet been discovered. Almost all the elements occurring in nature were discovered by the beginning of the twentieth century.

Atoms and Molecules

Greek thinker Democritus was convinced that bodies only seem to be solid, but in fact consist of the minutest particles. These particles are different in form for different bodies, but they are so small that they cannot be seen. That is why all bodies seem to us to be solid. Democritus called such very tiny particles which cannot be further divided and of which water and all other bodies consist atoms (derived from the Greek *atoms* meaning "indivisible"). This remarkable guess of ancient Greek thinkers born 24 centuries ago, was last long forgotten. Aristotle's erroneous teaching exercised complete sway over the scientific world for more than a thousand years. Asserting that all substances are mutually transmutable, Aristotle categorically denied the existence of atoms.[1]

In 1647, the Frenchman Pierre Gassendi (1592-1655) published a book in which he courageously denied Aristotle's teaching and asserted that all substances in the world consist of small indivisible particles-atoms. Atoms differ from each other in shape, size and mass. Agreeing with the teachings of the ancient atomists, Gassendi developed these teachings further. He explained how the millions of diverse bodies of nature can and do arise in the world. Nature can create thousands of the most diverse bodies from several tens of different atoms. Moreover in each body various atoms are united in small groups; Gassendi called these groups molecules, i.e. "small masses" (derived from the Latin *moles* meaning "mass"). Molecules of various bodies differ from each other in the number and kind ("sort") of atoms belonging to them. It is not difficult to understand that an immense number of different combinations of atoms, molecules can be united from several tens of different atoms. This is why there is such a great variety in the bodies surrounding us.[2]

However, Gassendi was incorrect when he believed that there were special atoms for heat, cold, taste and smell. According to Lomonosov molecules can be homogeneous or heterogeneous. In the former case, similar atoms are grouped in a molecule. In the latter, a molecule consists of atoms differing from each other. If somebody is composed of homogeneous molecules, it must be regarded as simple. If, on the contrary, a body consists of molecules built up from various atoms, Lomonosov calls it compound.

John Dalton (1766-1844) gave his famous atomic theory according to which atoms can neither be created nor destroyed. He believed that atoms cannot be divided. Later on it was proved that Dalton was wrong in his view on the indivisibility of atom. Later on it was proved that atoms can be divided into sub-atomic particles such as electron, proton and neutron.

States of Matter

The state of matter is determined by two circumstances: temperature and pressure. It is possible to obtain any substance in a solid, liquid and gaseous state or, as is also said, in a solid, liquid or gaseous phase.

Boiling

If we lower a thermometer into water which is kept for heating, the mercury level inches upwards and shows 100^{0}C. It means the water has reached its boiling point. The process of transforming water into stream requires energy. Let us compare the energy of a gram of water and a gram of the stream created out of. The molecules of the steam are distributed farther from each other than the water molecules. It is obvious that because of this the potential energy of the water will differ from that of the steam. The potential energy of attracting particles decreases as they approach. The energy of the steam is therefore greater than that of the water, and so the transformation of water into steam requires energy. This excess energy is imparted by the electric stove to the water boiling in the tea-kettle. Pressure influences the melting point of any substance. If the pressure is changed the melting point will also change. The influence of pressure on the melting point is much less than the analogous effect for boiling. The evaporation of solids is called *sublimation*. Naphthalene for example, is an evaporating solid. It melts at 80^{0}C, but evaporates at room temperature.

Molecular mechanics deals with the movements of molecules and transformation of matter from one state to another. The laws of thermodynamics belong to the basic laws of nature.

The Laws of Thermodynamics

The laws of thermodynamics define a group of physical quantities such as *temperature, energy* and *entropy,* that characterize *thermodynamic systems* in thermodynamic equilibrium. The laws also use various parameters for *thermodynamic processes,* such as *thermodynamic work* and *heat,* and establish relationships between them. They state *empirical facts* that form a basis of precluding the possibility of certain phenomena, such as *perpetual motion*. In addition to their use in *thermodynamics,* they are important fundamental *laws of physics* in general, and are applicable in other natural sciences.

Traditionally, thermodynamics has recognized three fundamental laws:

a) The first law of thermodynamics states that, when energy passes into or out of a system (as *work, heat* or *matter),* the system's *internal energy* changes in accord with the *law of conservation of energy*.

b) The second law of thermodynamics states that in a natural *thermodynamic process,* the sum of the entropies of the interacting thermodynamic systems never decreases. Another form of the statement is that heat does not spontaneously pass from a colder body to a warmer body.

c) The third law of thermodynamics states that a system's entropy approaches a constant value as the temperature approaches absolute zero C. With the exception of non-crystalline solids (glasses) the entropy of a system at absolute zero is typically close to zero.

The first and second laws prohibit two kinds of perpetual motion machines, respectively: the perpetual motion of the first kind which produces work with no energy input, and the *perpetual motion machine of the second kind* which spontaneously converts thermal energy into machine work.

What is quantum theory?

The word 'quantum' means 'a quantity' or a 'discrete amount'. On an every scale we are accustomed to the idea that the properties of an object such as its size, weight, colour, temperature, surface area, and motion are all qualities which can vary from one object to another in a smooth and continuous way. Apples, for example, come in all manner of shapes, sizes and colours without any noticeable gradations in between.

On the atomic scale, however things are very different. The properties of atomic particles such as their motion, energy and spin not always exhibit similar smooth variations, but may instead differ in discrete amounts. One of the assumptions of classical Newtonian mechanics was that the properties of matter are continuously variable. When physicists discovered that this motion breaks down on the atomic scale they had to devise an entirely new system of mechanics-quantum mechanics-to take account of the bumpiness which characterises the atomic behavior of matter. Quantum theory, then, is the underlying theory from which quantum mechanics is derived.

Considering the success of classical mechanics in describing the dynamics of everything from billiard balls to stars and planets, it is not surprising that its replacement by a new system of mechanics on the atomic scale was considered to be a revolutionary departure.

Quantum theory was proved by *Max Planck* in the year 1900 with the publication of a paper. His research was on the distribution of radiant heat energy from a hot body among various wave lengths. Under certain ideal conditions the energy is distributed in a characteristic way which Plank showed could only be explained by supposing that the electromagnetic radiation was emitted from the body in discrete packets or bundles, which he called *quanta*. The reason for this jerky behavior was unknown. Using quantum hypothesis Einstein successfully explained the so-called photoelectric effect in which light energy is observed to displace electrons from the surface metals.

Dualism of Matter

Dualism of matter was accepted by the world of science after the scientists observed the behavior of an object such as a *photon*. The photons exhibited both wave-like and particle-like properties. Photons can be made to produce diffraction and interference patterns, a sure test of their wave-like nature. On the other hand, in the photoelectric effect, photons knock elements out of metals. Here, the particle model of light seems to be more appropriate. Both wave and particle properties co-exist. The wave-particle dichotomy was not restricted to light. Physicists were concerned about the structure of atoms. In particular, they were puzzled by how electrons could go round and round a nucleus without emitting radiation, since it was known from Maxwell's electromagnetic theory that when charged particles move along curved paths they radiate electromagnetic energy.

If this were to occur continuously, the orbiting atomic electrons would rapidly lose energy and spiral into the nucleus.

In 1913 *Niels Bohr* proposed that atomic electrons are also 'quantized', in that they can reside without loss of energy in certain fixed energy levels.

When electrons jump between the levels, electromagnetic energy is released or absorbed in discrete quantities. These packets of energy are, in fact, photons.

By the mid 1920s a new system of mechanics-quantum mechanics-had been developed independently by *Erwin Schrödinger* and *Werner Heisenberg* to take account of this wave-particle duality. Quantum mechanics made possible developments in practical hardware, including the electron microscope, the laser and the transistor. No known experiments has contradicted the predictions of quantum mechanics in the last 60 years.[4]

Newtonian Deterministic Structure of the World

Newton believed that his mechanistic structure of the world was deterministic. For him both Space and time were absolute. His theory was rejected by Einstein. For Einstein space and time are not absolute. In fact it was not Space and Time, but Space-Time continuum. Einstein's Relativity theory questioned the deterministic theory of Newton. His special theory of Relativity focuses on the position of the observer as relative factor. For example if an individual's weight is 60 kg on the earth, he will weight only 12 kg on the moon because the gravitational force of the moon is 5 times less than that of the earth. In his General theory of Relativity Einstein proved that even sun rays bend due to the gravitation. Both Special Theory of Relativity and General Theory of Relativity proved the irrelevance of Newtonian mechanics in modern physics. Quantum mechanics replaced Newtonian mechanics. In Newtonian mechanics if we know the position and velocity of a physical body we can determine its future position. But such determinism is not certain in quantum mechanics. According to Quantum mechanics there is only *statistical probability* of the position of a physical body or an-electron. Moreover at the sub atomic level causality is irrelevant because we cannot locate a single cause for the movement of an electron. Different forces (causes) are causing an event to take place.

Causality and Statistical Physics

There are arguments to defend statistical laws of quantum mechanics as deterministic. But the defenders of determinism confuse with events of nature with determinism of a law. In case of events which are not occurrences of an individual ultimate particle (electron or quanta) but which involve a large collection of these particles, determinism may be said to operate as the law of probability ruling such events, and giving such high probabilities that they are practical certainties. But even in these cases we should not say that determinism strictly holds, as the fundamental law is statistical.[5]

L. Susan Stebbing thinks that in case of undetermined occurrences predictions can be made if large collection of them are involved in a process. 'In such a case, statistical law will be made in accordance with a deterministic procedure' Again, "It is clear that predictions can be made (i.e. inferences concerning what will happen) on the basis of statistical laws. Such predictions can never be *known* to be certainly true. But no predictions concerning the physical world can be known to be certainly true, since we have no logical ground for assuming that our extrapolations are correct".[6]

Now Stebbing does distinguish between a probable event and a probable conclusion, but she holds that determinism may be regarded as valid if there are laws (such as statistical laws) by means of which we can infer subsequent states from previous ones within precisely determined limits. Obviously, she holds that if in the case of statistical laws the logical ground for passing from an initial state to subsequent state is as sound as in the case of causal inference, which ground is what the logic of induction can offer for both kinds of laws, then determinism must be admitted as untouched by modern quantum physics. We admit that so far as the logical ground of predicting on the basis of a scientific law is concerned, no change has been brought about by quantum physics, the passing from ground to conclusion in an inductive syllogism in case of a statistical method of enquiry suffers from the same uncertainty as a similar passing in case of a causal method.[7] The conclusion in each case is a probable conclusion. According to Stebbing if causal laws are called determinate, statistical ones are equally so. But we must admit that statistical laws are applicable to the micro-world which is made up of large group of events in the micro-world as made up of large group of events in the micro-world as such a body of average size is made up of millions and millions of electrons. So we can say that statistical laws are indeterministic since they do not apply to single events. Causal laws apply to single events. Therefore they are deterministic.

Max Planck defends determinism in a way which is not essentially different from that of Stebbing. Some positivists mean by causal laws, some sort of simple laws and they include quantum physical statistical laws under causal laws. In a philosophical sense there is no contradiction between causal and statistical laws. This way of thinking stresses only the logical determinism involved in any kind of law and overlooks the difference between a law that applies to individual events or particles and a law that does so only to a crowd.[8]

Another kind of argument retains determinism in statistical law according to which statistical laws are based on causal laws. Russell also asserts that statistical laws assume strict causality as the basic law.[9] However Schrödinger's mechanics is indeterministic and statistical laws cannot be assumed to be causal laws. According to him in the case of a molecule (of classical kinetic theory) we could not know exactly and jointly the velocity and position, and so its initial conditions remain inexactly known with the result that predictions world become inaccurate.[10]

God Particle

The *Higgs boson* particle is called God particle because according to the theory laid out by Scottish physicist *Peter Higgs* and others in 1964, it is the physical proof of an *invisible, universe-wide field* that gave mass to all matter right after the Big Bang, forcing particles to coalesce into stars, planets and other celestial bodies. In 2012, scientists confirmed the detection of the long sought Higgs boson, also known as the "God particle". This particle helps give mass to all elementary particles that have mass, such as electrons, and protons. The elusive 'god particle' discovered by scientists in 2012 has the potential to destroy the universe, famed British physicist *Stephen Hawking* warned. According to Hawking at very high energy levels the Higgs boson, which gives shape and size to everything that exists could become unstable. The Higgs boson particle is so important as it causes an invisible energy field present throughout the universe.

Apart from atoms including electron, proton and neutron, the latest addition of God particle are the building blocks of the universe.

The Big Bang Theory

The Big Bang theory is the prevailing cosmological model explaining the existence of the observable universe from the earliest known periods through its subsequent large scale evolution. The model describes how the *universe expanded* from an initial state of high *density* and *temperature,* and offers a comprehensive explanation for a broad range of observed phenomena, including the abundance of light elements, the cosmic microwave background (CMB) radiation, and large-scale structure. Crucially, the theory is compatible with *Hubble-Lemaitre* law-the observation that the farther away a *galaxy is,* the faster it is moving away from Earth. The expansion of the universe and the movement of the galaxies have been experimentally verified. The *red shift* in the spectrometer is an indication that the galaxies are expanding away from the earth. Before Big Bang the cosmos reached a highly dense singularity. Detailed measurements of the expansion rate of the universe place the Big Bang singularity at around 13.8 billion years ago which is thus considered the age of the universe.

After its initial expansion, an event that is by itself often called the "Big Bang" the universe cooled sufficiently to allow the formation of *subatomic particles*, and later atoms. Giant clouds of these primordial elements mostly hydrogen, with some *helium* and *lithium*-later cloaked through *gravity* forming early stars and galaxies, the descendents of which are visible today. Besides these primordial building materials, astronomers observe the gravitational effects of an unknown *dark matter* surrounding galaxies. Most of the gravitational *potential* in the universe seems to be in this form and the Big Bang theory and various observations indicate that this excess gravitational potential is not created by *baryonic matter*, such as normal atoms. Measurements of the red shifts *supernovae* indicate that the expansion of the universe is accelerating, an observation attributed to *dark energy's* existence.

George Lemaitre first noted in 1927 that an expanding universe could be traced back in time to an originating, single point, which he called 'primeval' atom. *Edwin Hubble* confirmed through analysis of galactic *red shifts* in 1929 that galaxies are indeed drifting apart; this is important observational evidence for an expanding universe. For several decades, the scientific community was divided between supporters of the Big Bang and the rival *steady-state* model which both offered explanation for the observed expansion, but the steady-state model stipulated an eternal universe in contrast to the Big Bang's finite age. In 1964 the cosmologists were convinced that the steady-state theory was falsified, since unlike the *steady state* theory, the hot Big Bang predicted uniform background radiation throughout the universe caused by the high temperatures and densities in the distant past. A wide range of empirical evidence strongly favours the Big Bang, which is now essentially accepted.

Observable Universe

The observable universe is a ball shaped region of the universe comprising all matter that can be observed from Earth. The radius of visible universe: 46.508 billion light years. Contents: ordinary matter (baryonic)-4.9% Dark matter: 26.8%; Dark energy 68.3%. Density of total energy: $9.9{:}10^{-27}kg/m^3$ Mass (ordinary matter):1.5 10^{53}kg. The steady state cosmological model supported by Fred Hoyle, Thomas Gold and Hermann Bondi interpret the law of conservation of energy which is different from that of big bang theory. According to the steady state theory we have to calculate the *total amount* of matter present within the visible universe, i.e. matter present within the radius of 46.508 billion light years only. The matter present beyond the visible universe should not be calculated for total energy. However Lemaitre who supported Big Bang theory says that matter present even beyond 46.508 billion light years radius should also be taken for law of conservation of Energy. According to Law of conservation of energy matter can neither be created nor destroyed. But the steady state cosmologist says that a steady state of total amount of matter is maintained by continuously creating new matter. Due to expansion of the universe some matter will move away from the visible universe. So the loss of shifted matter is compensated by creating new matter. The Big Bang theory rejects the continuous creations of matter as held by the steady state cosmologist.

According to steady state cosmologists, the universe is *isotropic* and *homogeneous* in space and time. But according to Big Bang theory the universe is *isotropic* and homogeneous only in space and *not in time*. A steady state universe has no designing or end in time. The average density and arrangements of galaxies is the same.

Gravitation in the Theory of Big Bang

Gravity plays a starring role in the theory of the Big Bang, the immense expansion event from which the universe's billions of galaxies herald. According to Newton's law of universal gravitation, gravity is an attractive force that acts on every particle of matter in the universe. Without gravity the universe could not exist. The strength of gravitational attraction depends on *distance* and *mass*. If two particles of cosmic dust are close, they gravitate towards each other. Meanwhile, the gravitational force of a planet will pull on objects farther away. In the early twentieth century, Albert Einstein built on Newton's findings with his general theory of relativity which, among other things, explained gravity not as a force but as a distortion in the shape of space-time. A particularly massive object like a star warps both the time and space around it. Time itself passes measurably slower in close proximity to such an object and curves the otherwise straight path of speeding light waves. Gravity dictates the structure of the universe, from the way cosmic bodies form to the way they orbit more massive planets or *stars*. Einstein also proposed that the universe began as a singularity, a point with zero volume and infinity density containing all the matter of the universe. Then the Big Bang occurred, rapidly expanding all that matters with enough ferocity to overpower the inward pull of gravity. Einstein also predicted that we would be able to tell gravity was present during those early moments. All the resulting gas and dust eventually formed into the universe we know today due to gravity as well. Gravity is one of the four forces of nature, along with *electromagnetism*, strong force and weak force. The strong force and week forces work at the atomic level. The strong force holds the nucleus together and the weak force is responsible for *radio active decay*. Without these fundamental forces all matter in the universe would fall apart and float away. Subatomic particles exert electromagnetic forces on each other.

For example, positively charged protons could hold negatively charged electrons in orbit around the nucleus. Furthermore, electrons of one atom attracted protons of neighbouring atoms to form a residual electromagnetic force. Electromagnetism works both at macro and micro levels. Physicists believe that protons transmitted electromagnetic force over large distances. Theory related to electromagnetism at the atomic level is called the field of *Quantum electrodynamics* (QED). According to QED, photons transmit electromagnetic force both macroscopically and microscopically; however subatomic particles constantly exchange virtual photons during their electromagnetic interaction.

The Future of the Universe

After the Big Bang the universe exploded because of the primeval atom reaching critical density and began to expand. The expansion continued so that new galaxies and stars were born in the course of expansion. Will there be an infinite expansion or the expansion will stop? There are two forces at work: the force of expansion and the force of gravitation. There is a battle between dark energy and gravity as well as its density. As far as the future of the universe is concerned there are three possible fates for the universe. One is called the *Big crunch,* where gravity takes over and begins to pull the cosmos back, comprising to one point. Another extreme is the *Big Rip,* where the expansion of the universe just gets faster until galaxies, stars, planets, atoms and space itself is ripped apart. Somewhere between these two extremes is what the likely scenario where the expansion of the universe is not great enough for a big rip and gravity is not strong enough for a big crunch. Instead it will continue to expand, carrying everything we see today over the cosmic horizon where they will be so far away that their light cannot reach us. The sky will be dark and as all of the stars begin to go out, the universe will grow, cold and lifeless in a so called big freeze.

The first possibility of a future crunch or future Big Bang can be understood from the following graphical illustration:

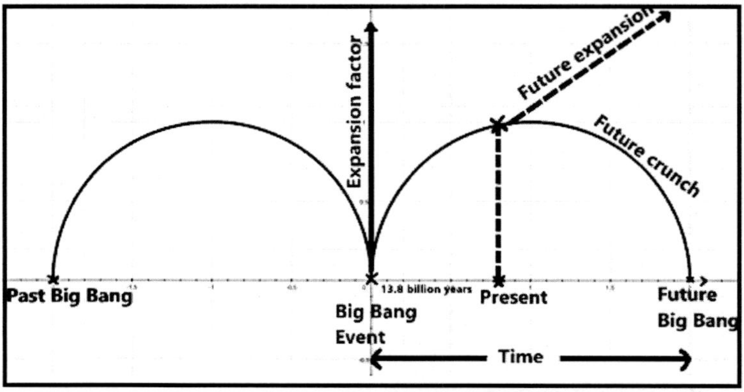

Spiral galaxy

Milky Way galaxy in which our solar system is a part

Spiral galaxy 55000 light years in diameter and 60 million light years from Earth

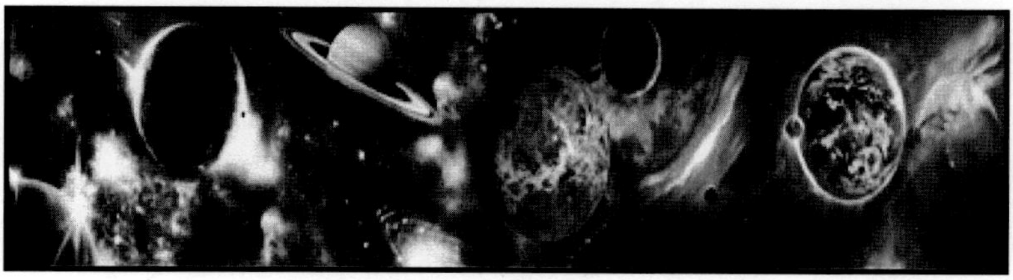

Solar System

Galaxies

A galaxy is a gravitationally bound system of stars, stellar remnants, interstellar gas, dust, and dark matter. The world is derived from the Greek *galaxias,* literally 'milky', a reference to the Milky Way galaxy that contains *solar system*. Galaxies range in size from *dwarfs* with just a few hundred million on (10^8) stars to *giants* with one hundred trillion (10^{14}) stars, each orbiting its galaxy's *centre of mass*.

Galaxies are categorised according to their visual *morphology* as *elliptical, spiral,* or *irregular*. Many are thought to have *supermassive black holes* at their centres. The Milky Way's central black hole, known as *Sagittarius A,* has a mass four million times greater than the sun. It has a *comoving distance* of 32 billion light years from Earth, and is seen as it existed just 400 million years after the Big Bang.

The space between galaxies is filled with the tenuous gas (the intergalactic medium) with an average density of less than one atom per cubic metre. Most galaxies are gravitationally organised into *groups, cluster* and *superclusters*. The Milky Way is part of the *Local Group,* which it dominates along with *Andromeda Galaxy.* Galaxies were formed after Big Bang (after 300000 years after the Big Bang). They were formed after the process of recombination from the atoms of *hydrogen* and helium-Nearly all the hydrogen was neutral (non-ionised) and readily observed light, and no stars had yet formed. As a result, this period has been called the "dark ages". It was from density fluctuation (or anisotropic irregularities) in this primordial matter that larger structures began to appear. As a result, masses of *baryonic* matter started to condense within cold dark matter halos. These primordial structures eventually became the galaxies we see today. The existence of galaxies so soon after the Big Bang suggests that *photo galaxies* must have grown in the so called "dark-ages". The light travelled from one part of the galaxy to reach the Earth does not take the same time as there is expansion of the universe. The creation of supermassive black holes appears to play a key role in actively regulating the growth of galaxies by limiting the total amount of additional matter added. During this early epoch, galaxies undergo a major burst of star formation. After two billion years the accumulated matter settles into a *galactic disc*. A galaxy will continue to absorb infalling material from high velocity clouds and dwarf galaxies throughout its life. This matter is mostly hydrogen and helium. The cycle of stellar birth and death slowly increases the abundance of heavy elements, eventually allowing the *formation of planets*. The galaxies collide with one another: As time passes merger of two systems of equal size is possible. Most bright galaxies have remained fundamentally unchanged for the last few billion years. The supply of stars-forming material is finite; once stars have converted the available supply of hydrogen into heavier elements, new star formation will come to an end. If there is *gravitational relaxation*, all stars will either fall into central supermassive black holes or be flung into intergalactic space as a result of collisions.

Black Holes

A black hole is a region of space time where gravity is so strong that nothing-no particles or even electromagnetic radiation such as light-can escape from it. The theory of general relatively of Einstein predicts that a sufficiently compact mass can deform space time to form a black hole. The *boundary* of no escape is called *event horizon*. Although it has a great effect on the fate and circumstances of an object crossing it, it has no locally detectable features according to general relativity.[11]

In many ways, a black hole acts like an ideal black body, as it reflects no light. Moreover, *quantum field theory in curved space time* predicts that event horizons emit *Hawking radiation,* with the *same spectrum* as a black body of a temperature inversely proportional to its mass. This temperature is of the order of billionth of *Kelvin* for *Stellar black holes,* making it impossible to observe directly.

Objects whose gravitational fields are too strong for light to escape were first considered by John Michael and Pierre-Simon Laplace. In 1916, Karl Schwarzschild formed the first modern solutions of general relativity that would characterise a *black hole.* David Finkelstein in 1958, first published the interpretation of *"black hole"* as a region of space from which nothing can escape.

Black holes of stellar mass form when massive stars collapse at the end of their life cycle. After a black hole has formed, it can grow by absorbing mass from its surroundings. Supermassive black holes exist in the centres of most galaxies. The presence of a black hole can be inferred through its interaction with other *matter* and with electromagnetic radiation such as visible light. Any matter that falls onto a black hole can form an external *accretion disk* heated by *friction,* forming *quasars,* some of the brightest object in the universe. Stars passing too close to a supermassive black hole can be shredded into steamers that shine very brightly before being "swallowed". If other stars are orbiting a black hole, their orbits can determine the black hole's mass and location. Such observations can be used to exclude possible alternations such as neutron stars. In this way astronomers have identified numerous stellar black hole candidates in *binary systems* and established that the radio source known as "Sagittarius A" at the core of the Milky Way galaxy, contains a supermassive black hole of about 4.3 million *solar* masses. As of 2021, the nearest known body thought to be a black hole is around 1500 light years away from us. Though only two dozen black holes have been found so far in the Milky Way, there are thought to be hundreds of millions, most of which are solitary and do not cause emission of radiation. Therefore they would only be detectable by *gravitational lensing*. A black hole, after formation has there independent physical properties: mass, electric charge and angular momentum; the black hole is otherwise featureless. A charged black hole repels other like charges just like any other charged object.

Black holes can be classified as :1) super massive black hole, 2) intermediate mass black hole, 3) stellar black hole, and 4) micro black hole.

The singularity at the centre of a black hole is the ultimate no man's land: a place where matter is compressed down to an infinitely tiny point, and all conceptions of time and space completely breakdown.

Atomic Theory of Vaisheshika

Vaisheshika is one of the six schools of Indian philosophy from ancient India. In its early stages the *Vaisheshika* was an independent philosophy with its own metaphysics, epistemology, logic, ethics and soteriology. Over time, the Vaisheshika system became similar in its philosophical procedures, ethical conclusions and soteriology to the *Nyaya* school of Hinduism, but retained its difference in epistemology and metaphysis. The *Vedas* were the scriptures for the Vaisheshika. The school is known for its insights in *naturalism*. It is a form of *atomism* in natural philosophy. It postulated that all objects in the physical universe are reducible to *paramanu* (*atoms*), and one's experience are derived from the interplay of substance (a function of atoms, their number and their spatial arrangements), quality, activity, commonness, particularity and inherence. Everything was composed of atoms, qualities emerged from aggregates of atoms, but the aggregation and nature of these atoms was predetermined by cosmic forces. *Ajivaka metaphysics* included a theory of atoms which was later adopted in the Vaisheshika school. According to the Vaisheshika school, knowledge and liberation were achieved by a complete understanding of the world of experience.

Vaisheshika darshana was founded by Kanada Kashyapa around the sixth to second century BCE.

The Atomic Theory

According to the Vaisheshika school, the *trasarenu* are the smallest *mahat* (perceivable) particles and defined as *tryanukas* (triads). These are made of three parts, each of which are defined as *dvyanuka* (dyad). The *dvyanukas* are conceived as made of two parts, each of which are defined as *paramanu* (atom). The *paramanus* (atoms) are indivisible and eternal; they can neither be created nor destroyed. Each *paramanu* (atom) possesses its own distinct (*vis'esa*) individuality and has an inhering relation which is responsible for change and motion. The measure of the partless atoms is known as *parimandalaparimanu*. It is eternal and it cannot generate the measure of any other substance.

Philosophical atomism is a reductive argument proposing not only that everything is composed of atoms and void, but that nothing they *compose* really exists: the only things that really exist are *atoms*. The atoms are integrated *mechanically* in an otherwise empty void. Atomism stands in contrast to a *substance theory* wherein a prime material continuum remains qualitatively invariant under division (for example, the ratio of the four *classical elements* would be the same in any portion of homogeneous material. Indian Buddhists such as *Dharmakirti* (sixth or seventh century CE) and others developed distinctive theories of atomism, for example involving momentary (*ksanikavada*) atoms that flash in and out of existence.

Kanada's *Vaisheshika Sutra*, gives a detailed account of the creation and existence of the universe using naturalistic atomism, applying logic and realism, and is one of the earliest known systematic realist *ontology* in human history. The text discusses motions of different kind and laws that govern it, the meaning of *dharma*, a theory of epistemology, the basis of *Atman* and the nature of *yoga* and *moksha*. The explicit mention of motion as the cause of all phenomena in the world and several propositions about it makes it one of the earliest texts on physics.

Kanada's *Vaisheshika Sutra* defines and describes three categories and their causal aspects: substance, quality and action. It explains their differences, similarities and relationships between these three. It also defines and explains a universal, a particular (*visesa*) and their hierarchical relationship. Kanada states that it is from combination of particulars that some universals emerge. In the second chapter of the *Vaisheshika Sutras* Kanada presents five substances (earth, air, water, fire, space) each with a distinct quality: He argues that all except "air" and "space" is verifiable by perception, while existence of invisible air is established by inference (air blows, and that there must be a substance that affects the touch sensation to the skin; space is inferred from one's ability to move from one point to another unhindered – a point he revises in later part of the text by asserting that sound is perceived and proves space).

In the third chapter Kanada states his views on Atman and in the fourth chapter about the body and its adjuncts. The fifth chapter discusses about *yoga* and *moksha* and the sixth chapter deals with ethics. Measurement and its importance is dealt with in the eighth chapter. The ninth chapter deals with the nature of cognition and in the tenth chapter he discusses epistemology. The eleventh chapter deals with his views on soul, *karma* and meditation as a means to soul knowledge.

Criticism of Big Bang and Steady-state Theories

According to Bhaskaranand Tripathi, both Big Bang and Steady state theories are mere hypotheses and nothing ensures their correctness about formation of universe. The theory of Sankhya philosophy is far better than these two said theories. The Sankhya system says that nothing was there before the formation of universe except the three attributes called. *Sattva, Rajas* and *Tamas*. All these three attributes were in a position of equilibrium. The basic tendency of each attribute was to subside the others. This overcoming tendency of each attribute incidentally culminated in a big bang due to a state of un equilibrium: The being is sounded as O>>>>M (OUM). This sound is still echoing and the universe is still spreading as the sound is spreading. These three attributes were the main cause of formation of the sky, the nature the water and the beings in water after billions of years that paved the way for evolution. The Sankhya system also tells us how the air, the sound, the mind, and the ego like attributes came into being.

Indian Theories of Universe

How did the ancient Indians view the cosmos, time and life? Subhash Kak tells us about the Indian cyclical model and ideas related to time. It is generally known that the Indians believed in a cyclic universe. This idea is related to three other beliefs: i) time is endless and space has infinite extension; ii) earth is not the centre of the universe; and iii) laws govern all development, including the creation and destruction of the universe. It was believed that there are connections between the physical and the physiological worlds, and an equivalence existed between the outer cosmos and the inner cosmos of the individual. This is expressed in the famous sentence:

"Yatpinde tad brahmande"

"as in the cell so in the universe"

The Indian cyclic model assumes the existence of countless island universes, which go through their own periods of development and destruction. The conception of cyclicity is taken to be recursive. For an early exposition of these astronomical and cosmological ideas, one may like to read *Al Biruni's* classic history of Indian science composed in 1030 CE, and for an even earlier, popular view of Indian ideas, one may consult the great Vendantic text called the *Yoga Vasishtha*. This work was composed in Srinagar over a thousand years ago and concerns the young Rama who is disillusioned with life getting instruction from the Sage Vasishtha over a period of 21 days. The narrative is in terms of intertwined stories and it contains romance, deepest philosophy, magic, realism and adventure.

Cyclic Periods

The basic period is *kalpa,* the "day" of *Brahma,* which is 4.32 billion years long. There is an equally long "night", and 360 such "days" and "nights". The life of Brahma is 100 such years, which is thus 3,11,040 billion years long. Then there exist longer periods in an endless process.

Sub-Periods

Within the *kalpa* are fourteen cycles of local creation and destruction called *manvantaras,* each lasting 306.720 million years. Each of these period is to be taken to be a period of local destruction (extinction) and subsequent regeneration. Within each *manvantara* are 71 smaller cycles, called *mahayugas*. These periods are described by *Aryabhatta,* the great astronomer born in 476 CE. As is generally known, *Aryabhatta* presented the rotation information of the outer planets with respect to the sun, meaning that his system was partially *heliocentric;* furthermore, he considered the earth to be rotating on its own axis. In another version, described in the *Suryasiddhanta* and the *puranas,* each *Kalpa* equals 1000 *yugas* of 4.32 million years. Yoga Vasishtha says that directions depend on the position of the poles, the moments of the stars, the sun and the moon, and that the directions change from one sub-period to another.

Al-Biruni

Al-Biruni says about the Indian conception of time thus:

> "The Hindu's have divided duration into two periods, a periods of motion, which has been determined as time, and a period of rest, which can only be determined in an imaginary way according to the analogy of that which has first been determined, the period of motion. The Hindus hold the eternity of the *creator* to be *determinable,* not measurable, since it is *infinite.* They do not, by the word *creation,* understand a formation of *something* out of *nothing.* They mean by creation only the working with a piece of clay, and making such arrangements with it as will lead to certain ends and aims which are potentially in it."

Island Universes

The universe is split up into many island-universes, as describe in the:

Yoga Vasishtha

I saw countless creations though they did not know of one another's existence. Some were coming into being, others were perishing, all of them had different shielding atmospheres [from five to thirty six atmospheres]. There were different elements in each, they were in different stages of evolution. In some there was apparent natural order in others there was utter disorder, in some there was no light and hence no time-sense.

Evolution

The idea of evolution is basic to all Indian thought. The *Samkhya* is the Indian theory of evolution, which is supposed to apply both to the individual and the cosmos. In it, the basic entities are pure consciousness (*purusha*) and materiality (*prakriti*). The *prakriti* (nature) has three constituent qualities (*gunas*) called *sattva, rajas* and *tamas* and as the balance between these three changes, the universe evolves. Out of the interplay of the five basic elements arise other principles (*tattvas*): five subtle elements, five action senses, five senses of perception, mind, egoity and intellect. The evolutionary sequence goes through many levels. The *tattvas* help in the emergence of life out of inert matter. The *gunas* are not to be taken as abstract principles alone. Indian thought believes that structure in nature is recursive, and the *gunas* show up in various forms at different levels of expression.

The texts imply that ingredients for the growth of life are available throughout the universe. Infinite numbers of universes are conceived, so each new one is created like a bubble in an ocean of bubbles. The *tattvas* are not discrete and their varying expression creates the diversity of life in and across leading different species. Each sensory and motor *tattva* is mapped into a corresponding organ. Indian thought conceives of 8.4 million species, which number is impressive, considering that modern authorities (such as Dan Graur and Wen-Hsiung Li in their *Fundamentals of Molecular Evolution*, (p. 436) estimate the number of extant species to be 4.5-10 million.

The physicist Erwin Schrödinger thought that the *Sankhyan tattvas* were the most plausible model for the evolution of the sensory organs. A quote on evolution on earth from the *Yoga Vasishtha*:

I remember that once upon a time there was nothing on this Earth, neither trees and planets, nor even mountains. For a period of eleven thousand years (4 million Earth years) the Earth was under *lava* ... Later apart from the polar region, the rest of the Earth was covered by water. And then forests enveloped the Earth, and great *asuras* (demons) ruled. Then there arose great mountains, but without any human inhabitants. For a period of ten thousand years (almost 4 million Earth years) the Earth was covered with the corpses of the *asuras*.

Yoga Vasishtha also speaks of minor ages of destruction on Earth that correspond to the Yugas.

Evolution of Life

The Indians believed that all life can be divided into three classes: (*Chandogya Upanisad* 6.3.1)

In truth, beings have here three kinds of seeds, born from the egg, born alive and born from the germ. The ancient Indians believed that life on other planets exists and that there was a gradual rise of life on the earth. This belief implies a panspermia theory.

Inner Cosmos

In Indian mythology, the continents are in concentric circles. Wrongly applied to the outer cosmos, this *pauranic* cosmology represents the inner cosmos of the individual that maps the universe. It therefore brings in outer astronomy only in an incidental fashion. The earth of the *Puranas* is the individual pictured as the plane that touches the navel. Below the navel are the underworld; above the navel are the sun and the moon in the head, and beyond them the planets and the stars. The perceived dimensions of the sun and the moon in this conception relate to the inner cosmos.

Hinduism and the Universe

For Hindus the universe was created by Brahma, the creator who made the universe out of himself. After Brahma created the world, it is the power of *Vishnu* which preserves the world and human beings. As part of the cycle of birth life and death it is *Shiva* who will ultimately destroy the universe. As far the origin of the universe Hindus believe that a lotus flower grew from Lord Vishnu's navel with Brahma sitting on it. Brahma separated the flower into three parts-the heavens, the Earth and the sky. He works with Lord Vishnu and Lord Shiva to maintain an un ending cycle of universe. All three are aspects of Brahma.

Time is not a straight line. Instead there are external cycles with universe being created, existing and dying followed by recreation, existence and death. There is no beginning and no end. This is mirrored in the belief in reincarnation.

Solar System and Hindu Beliefs

The solar system is the gravitationally bound system of the sun and the objects that orbit it. It formed 4.6 billion years ago from the gravitational collapse of a giant interstellar molecular cloud. The vast majority of the system's mass is in the sun, with most of the remaining mass contained in the planet *Jupiter*. The four *inner system* planets-*Mercury, Venus, Earth* and *Mars*– are terrestrial planets, being composed primarily of rock and metal. The four *giant planets* of the *outer system* are substantially larger and more massive than the terrestrials. The two *largest Jupiter* and *Saturn* are gas giants, being composed mainly of hydrogen and helium; the next two, *Uranus* and

Neptune, are *ice* giants, being composed mostly of *volatile* substance with relatively high melting points compared with hydrogen and helium, such as water, *ammonia,* and *methane.* All eight planets have nearly circular orbits that lie near the plane of Earth's orbit called the *ecliptic.*

The solar magnetic science is that branch of science of astronomy which deals with the special dynamic centre of bodies within our solar system. These bodies influence the birth and growth and progress of everything that exists upon the face of the earth. The Chinese, Egyptians and Hindus had their own versions of astronomical studies. Our ancients believed that the stars rule the destiny of people. That idea existed among all the ancient nations, and so they studied the movements of the stars and planets, thinking that they would discover the law which controls human destiny. It became almost a part of their religion and was known as astrology. The Chaldean, the Egyptian, the Babylonian and the Hindu priests were all astrologers. In the Vedas one of the six limbs of the scriptures (*sadangas*) was astronomy.

Hindu Beliefs

The Hindu astronomers brought the influence of the stars in minute details in all the affairs of life especially in the marriage and other religious ceremonies. Even today astronomy and astrology are the strongest features in India. Their almanac contains all the prophesies and foretelling of events which are connected with our earthly life. For instance if we want to build a home we are supposed to lay the foundation of our home at an auspicious moment and that auspicious moment must be according to the position of the planets and the position of the earth and signs of the zodiac and so on. The marriage ceremony could not be held without consulting the horoscope of the bride and the groom. Parents are very particular about the wedding. The date of the wedding should be fixed by the astronomers, and all these are very strictly observed. When one would move from one house to another, he would not move any day as he likes without consulting astronomers; or when any particular enterprise is made, that should be in perfect harmony with the conditions of the planets. This part of astronomy is called *Phalita-jyotisha,* which literally means influence of planets on practical life.[12]

The Hindu and the Egyptian astronomers gave the name zodiac to the belt of the celestial sphere eight degrees across on each side of the ecliptic and divided it into twelve parts of thirty degrees each, called the signs and gave a fanciful name to each: *Aries, Taurus, Gemini, Cancer, Leo, Virgo, Libra, Scorpio, Sagittarius, Capricorn, Aquarius* and *Pisces*. The Zodiac's 360^0 is divided into 12 parts (30^0each) and each part is given a name. The whole being of man may be compared to a psychometer. It is psychometrically related to the solar system and is particularly sensitive to the planetary vibrations which affect our earth on account of their relative positions. Like attracts like. The positive pole of the human body is attracted to the positive pole of the zodiac. A man born in Aries is positive, intellectual and active in mental pursuits. Inventive geniuses are born under the influence of Aries, because Aries is the head. They prefer intellectual to physical pursuit. On account of this tremendous mental activity, it is called also a fire sign and so Aries can be known as the fire sign. Similarly different signs influence human beings with different characteristics. So principal parts of the human body can be influenced at different signs of the zodiac when the planets are in favourable or unfavourable position. If they are favourably accepted, then the result is good, but if they are unfavourably accepted, the result is bad. Virgo rules over our stomach, liver and kidneys. Virgo has influence over these organs. It makes one emotional, spiritual and religious. It has a good influence over our physical and mental conditions. Scorpio is a negative pole. Sagittarius governs the part of the leg above the knees, which is called thigh. The hands and fingers will come to Capricorn. If there be any bad aspect in Sagittarius, rheumatism would be the result.

Thus by studying solar anatomy we can tell the various causes of diseases and can diagnose them by studying the positions and various aspects of the planets and the earth. Heliocentric science is based upon the perfect harmony between the earth and celestial bodies. We can imagine a gigantic being of the universe with his head in Aries and his feet at Pisces. This celestial body is the original man of the zodiac, every part of which is represented by the twelve signs of the zodiac and also by the physical body of men and animals. And there is also harmony among them. Every part of sign that is described in the zodiac, is a ruler of a certain part of the body. The part of the body in a human being or in an animal is influenced by the sign, and that is the correspondence.

Indian tradition admits reincarnation of the individual souls. It does not take place all of a sudden. The soul is waiting for an opportunity and those souls that are advanced spiritually, can be conscious of those conditions, but with ordinary mortals that consciousness may not exist. They are unconsciously drawn towards such conditions; or in other words, they gravitate. That gravitation again is guided by the *law of karma,* of action and reaction by thoughts and deeds of previous lives. So, when we come to this planet, we are not only in perfect harmony with the planetary conditions with the influence of the signs of the zodiac, but also we are governed by thoughts and deeds of our previous lives. How this wonderful harmony is regulated is a great mystery.[13]

Soul and Universe

Scientists account of the universe and its evolution after Big Bang is mechanical, physical and purposeless. Vedanta believes in the existence of Absolute spirit as the ultimate Reality. It believes that man need not be a slave to the physical conditions of the planetary influence. It teaches that the will of the human beings is all powerful and if you hold the thought and bring out the soul's power, you will be able to overcome the natural influences. The power of *Atman* or the soul is greater than that of the solar system. The soul is a part of the omnipotent and divine being, and it has absolute power to change all the natural or phenomenal conditions, no matter how the planets are against you. If you can send your vibrations, i.e. soul vibrations, which are no other than the spiritual forces, then that will overcome all these planetary influence.

If an astrologer would cast our horoscopes he would say, "These are the conditions, but there is a way out of it, and we can overcome these conditions by performing the spiritual practices or observing spiritual laws". We should remember that the power of the soul is greater than the power of the solar system. Because one is the material of the phenomenal world, including the earth and the heaven, whereas the other is concerned with the spirit, which animates but transcends the limit of the world and makes a man God-man. We should remember that we are the immortal soul inspite of the changing covering of our material body and we can create our conditions and destiny. We can overcome these planetary influences by our good thoughts and can immortalise ourselves by realizing the soul of the planetary systems which is the immortal *Atman*. This Vedanta interpretation of our solar system is reflected in Richmond's book on *Religion of the universe*, which teaches both science of the universe and the science of the soul.

Jain Theory of Universe

Jains believes that the universe we preserve really exists and is not an illusion. It contains two classes of thing-Jivas-living souls, and *ajivas*-non-living objects, which include everything else, including space. Nothing in the universe is ever destroyed or created, they simply change from one form to another.

Jains believe that the universe has always existed and will always exist. It is regulated by cosmic laws and kept going by its over energy process. This concept of the universe is compatible with scientific thinking.

Jains do not believe that the universe was created by God. The Jaina word that comes closest to the western idea of the universe is "*loka*". The loka is the framework of the universe. It contains the world we experience at the moment as well as the worlds of heaven and hell.

The loka exists in space. Space is infinite, the universe is not.

The Nature of the Universe

The Jain universe is in five parts:

(i) *The supreme abode*:

The region where liberated beings live forever.

(ii) *The upper world*:

The region where celestial beings live, but not for ever.

(iii) *The middle world:*

The region where human beings live. This is the only part of the universe from which a being can achieve enlightenment.

(iv) *The lower world:*

This region consists of seven hells where beings are tormented by demons and by each other. The torment does not last forever.

(v) *The base:*

The region where the lowest forms of life live.

(vi) *Time:*

Jains regard historical time as cyclical. The universe moves through lengthy eras of time which Jains usually describe as like the serious of downward and upward moments of a point on the rim of a turning wheel. The downward movement is called *avasarpini* and the upward movement is called as *utsarpini*. Each full turn of the wheel is called *kalpa*. Each cycle is divided into 6 ages represented by spokes. The

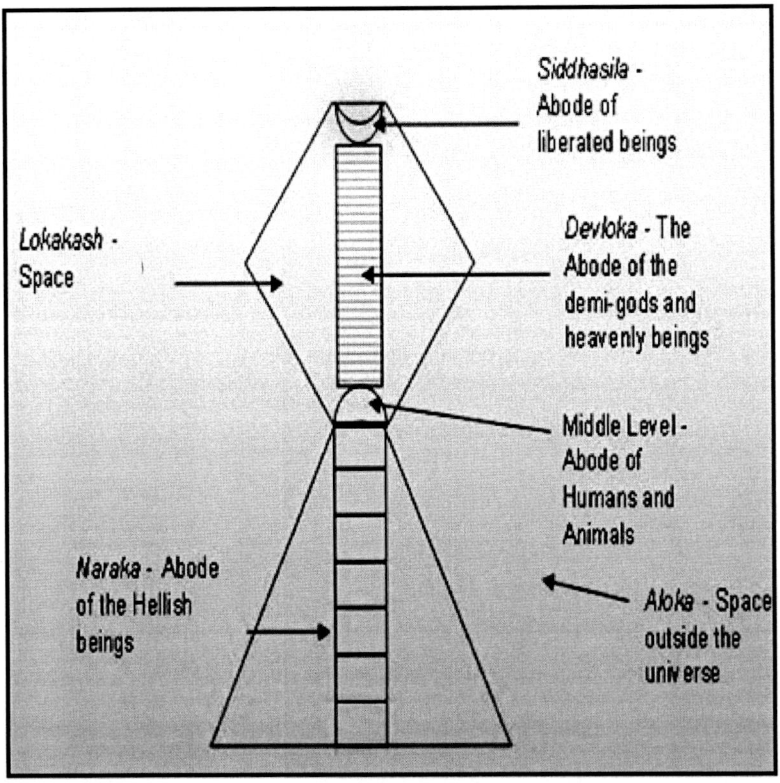

The Jain Universe

first three spokes of a downward cycle are a golden age after which conditions decline until Jainism dies out in the sixth spoke. This is reversed in the following upward cycle, and so on. Each full turn of the wheel take a very long time: effectively an infinity-long enough for the lives of 24 *tirthankaras.*

The Jains believe in *dravyas* (substances). They are called *astikaya.* All forms of substance except space are confined within the *loka* (universe).

The categories of substance are:

Jiva, Dharma, Adharma Pudgala, Akasha and *Kala*

References

1. L.D. Landau and A.I. Kitaigorodsky, *Molecules,* Mir Publishers, Moscow, 1986, pp. 12-13.
2. *Ibid.*
3. P.C.W. Davies and J.R. Brown, *The Ghost in the Atom: A Discussion of the Mysteries of Quantum Physics,* Cambridge University Press, London, 1993, pp. 1-4.
4. P.K. Sengupta, *Pravas Jivan Chaudhury on Multi-aspects of Philosophy,* Indian Council of Philosphical Research, New Delhi, 2003, p. 161.
5. *Ibid.,* p. 161.
6. L. Susan Stebbing, *Philosophy and the Physicists,* Dover Publications, New York, p. 209.
7. Julius W. Friend and James Fieblemann, *What Science Really Means,* Creative Media Partners, LLC, 2021, p. 187.
8. P.K. Sengupta, *op. cit.,* p. 164.
9. Bertrand Russell, *Determinism and Physics,* University of Durham Philosophical Society, 1936, p. 16.
10. Schrödinger, *Science and Human Temperament,* George Allen & Unwin Ltd., London, 1934.

11. In Einstein's *General theory of relativity,* gravitation is the relative factor whereas in his *special theory* of relativity position of the observer is the relative factor.

12. Swami Abhedananda, *A Study of Heliocentric Science,* Ramakrishna Vedanta Math, Kolkata, 2011, p. 97.

13. *Ibid.,* pp. 110-111.

Chapter IX

Scientific Explanation

There are events taking place around us. These events take evoke curiosity in us and therefore naturally we ask "why at all the events are taking place the way we observe them? The common man can explain the events from his own perspective. But the scientific explanations are different from the explanations of the common-sense. Scientific explanations not only explain the present occurrence of events but also *predict* the future occurrence of events. Some philosophers of science find a symmetry between *explanation* and *prediction*. But there are some who oppose such a symmetry between explanation and prediction. Those who hold the symmetry thesis believe that scientific explanation not only explains the present occurrence of events but also *control* the future events. Explanation of events and description of events are not the same. Those who describe the occurrence of events merely describe the 'state of affairs' and don't go beyond it. Empirical phenomena which are explained can be classified as: a) Physical b) Biological and c) Social. The methodology adopted to explain the physical phenomena is not the same as the methodologies to be followed to explain Biological and Social Phenomena. The explanations offered by the scientists will also be questioned by the emergent evolutionists like Lloyd Morgan. According to the emergent theory, the constituents of objects will lead to the 'emergence' of 'novelties' and hence the explanation is inadequate. The explanation must incorporate the novel qualities of the objects for better understanding of the events around us. In scientific explanation the case to be explained is called *Explanandum* and the premises or the statements such as laws from which explanation is deduced is called *Explanans*. There is a logical relation between Explanans and Explanandum. The Explanation of individual events is different from the explanation of scientific laws. Inductive and Deductive are the two patterns of Explanations. Inductive pattern is invariably connected to the probabilistic kind of Explanation. There are many kinds of deductive patterns of Explanation.[1]

Hempel's Covering-Law Model

The covering-law model of scientific explanation explains an event by reference to another event. It necessarily presupposes an appeal to laws or general propositions correlating events of the type to be explained (explananda) with events of the type cited as its causes or conditions (explanans). It is rooted in David Hume's doctrine that, when two events are said to be causally related, all that is meant is that they instantiate certain regularities of succession that have been repeatedly observed to hold between such events in the past. This doctrine was given more rigorous expression by the logical positivist Carl Hempel (1905-1997). Hempel's covering-law model is also known as the *deductive-nomological model* (DN model) of scientific explanation. The DN model poses scientific explanation as a deductive structure, one where truth of its premises entails truth of its conclusion, hinged on phenomenon to be explained. The term *deductive* distinguishes the DN model's intended *determinism* from the probabilism of inductive inferences. The term nomological is derived from the Greek nomos meaning "law".

In the DN model, a law *axiomatises* an *unrestricted generalisation* from antecedent A to consequent B by conditional propositions-If A, then B-and has empirical content testable. A law differs from mere true regularity. The phenomenon to be explained is the explanandum – an event, law, or theory-where as the premises to explain it are *explanans*, true or highly confirmed, containing at least one *universal law*, and entailing the explanandum. Thus, given the explanans as initial, specific conditions C_1, C_2,……Cn Plus general laws L_1, L_2,……Ln, the phenomenon E as explanandum is a deductive consequence thereby scientifically explained

$C_1, C_2, \ldots\ldots Cn$

$L_1, L_2, \ldots\ldots Ln$

$\therefore E$

Within the class of true generalisations, we may distinguish between those that are only "accidentally true" and those that are "laws". To use Hempel's examples, the generalisation

1)All members of the Greensburg School Board for 1964 are bald is, if true, only accidentally so. In contrast

2)All gases expand when heated under constant pressure, is a law. Thus according to the DN model, the latter generalisation can be used, in conjunction with information that some particular sample of gas has been heated under constant pressure, to explain why it has expanded. By contrast, the former generalization (1) in conjunction with the information that a particular person 'n' is a member of the 1964 Greensbury school board, cannot be used to explain why 'n' is bald.

As an additional illustration of a DN explanation of a particular event, consider a derivation of the position of Mars at some future time from Newton's laws of motion, the Newtonian inverse square law governing gravity and information about the mass of the sun, the mass of Mars and the present position and velocity of each. In this derivation the various Newtonian laws figure as essential premises and they are used, in conjunction with appropriate information about initial conditions (the masses of Mars and the Sun and so on), to derive the explanandum (the future position of Mars) via a deductively valid argument. The DN criteria are thus satisfied

Inductive Statistical Explanation

The DN model is meant to capture explanation via deduction from deterministic law and this raises the obvious question of the explanatory status of statistical laws. Do such laws explain at all, and if so, what do they explain and under what conditions? Hempel distinguishes two varieties of statistical explanation. The first of these, *deductive-statistical* (DS) explanation involves the deduction of "a narrower statistical uniformity from a more general statistical law. Since DS explanation involves deduction of the *explanandum* from a law, it conforms to the same general pattern as the DN explanation of regularities. However, in addition to DS explanation, Hempel also recognises a distinctive sort of statistical explanation, which he calls *inductive-statistical* or IS explanation. In IS explanation, the relation between explanans and explanandum is, in Hempel's words, "inductive" rather than deductive-hence the name inductive-statistical explanation.

Symmetry and Asymmetry in Explanation

In the case of explanation of an event E when there are certain conditions present at time 't_1', when in future similar conditions present at time 't_2', but the event is not taking place there is a kind of asymmetry between explanation and prediction. For example for 'cough' if one takes a particular medicine at time 't_1' and if the cough stops, but at time t_2 the same medicine does not stop cough we say that there is asymmetry between explanation and prediction. But when we throw a stone and if it falls on the ground we say it is due to gravitational force-we try to explain the stone falling on the ground through Newton's law of gravitation. In this case there is symmetry between the present and the future events.

Prediction, Retrodiction and Post-diction

In the case of prediction we predict an event E at time t_2 based on the evidence from time t_1. For example we predict rain based on our experience of seeing the formation of dark clouds in the sky. The relation between cloud and rain holds good for the future rain too because we have the experience of the rain in the present time or in the past. Therefore for prediction we proceed from the present evidence to the occurrence of future event. In the case of *retrodiction* we *infer* the occurrence of the event in the past based on the evidence in the present. For example we infer the past rain on seeing wetness on the ground in the present. Such an inference is based on the evidence collected in the present. In the case of post-diction we infer an occurrence of an event E at time t_1, the data for which was collected at time t_2 for the event which had taken place at time t_3. For example we say it is post-diction if we infer (and make statement) in the year 1996 CE based on the evidence collected in the year 1921 CE, for the event occurred in 1000 BCE. The Mohenjo-daro-Harappa civilization which is said to have flourished more than 3000 years ago came to light when archaeologists collected data in Pakistan in the beginning of the twentieth century. The data was studied and through carbon dating method the statement of the findings was made at a later data. In this case the Indus Valley civilization (the period) which flourished at time t_1, the data collected at time t_2 and the inference was made at time t_3.

Patterns of Scientific Explanation

There are two patterns of scientific explanation: Inductive and deductive.

Ernest Nagel enumerates four kinds of explanation: 1) Deductive 2) Probabilistic 3) Teleological and4) Genetic.[2]

Deductive Explanation

In the deductive kind of explanation the *Explanans* is a universal law from which explanation is deduced for an *explanandum*. Ex. Why the addition of the odd numbers always ends up with a square?

1, 3, 5, 7, 9, 11…

$1=1^2$

$1+3=2^2$, $1+3+5=3^2$, $1+3+5+7=4^2$, etc…

Here the *explanandum* is explained from an *Explanans* which is a universal law of Mathematics

Probabilistic Explanation

In the case deductive explanation, the explanation is deduced from the Explanans which is an invariably established law of science. The empirical validity of the premise is not verified. The validity of the *explanandum* has the observational element. But in the probabilistic explanation there is a 'jump' from some cases to all cases, i.e. from 'particular' to 'universal'.

Inductive generalization is interpreted as probabilistic explanation. When there is a jump from some to all or from particular to universal there is only 'inference' and not 'certainly'. Ex. When we observe clouds causing rain in the 'present', we 'predict' that there will be rain preceded by clouds. But sometimes there may be clouds not followed by rain. In this circumstance we have to admit that there is no necessary relation between clouds and rain. Similarly, if a physician prescribes a drug for a particular ailment, the drug may *probably* cure the ailment in future. We cannot say that there is certainty for the future occurrence of events. Therefore probabilistic explanation does not support a necessary relation between explanation and prediction.[3]

Teleological Explanation

Empirical statements which are 'purposive' are called teleological statements. "why do we have lungs? The answer should give the purpose of the lungs in the body-the inhalation of air so that oxygen can be utilised in blood circulation. Similarly all parts of our body have specific functions to perform. The teleological or functional aspect is relevant not only to the part of our body but also to several natural or artificial objects around us. These objects have got specific functions to perform. In certain cases the purpose will be achieved in future. The growth of paddy crops will lead to the yield of the grains of paddy. Therefore, the 'biological development' of paddy crop is in the process of achieving a purpose. However we cannot say that any biological process will lead to only one purpose. Same biological function may lead to achieving several purposes. A particular structure has the function for a particular purpose. However, the same purpose can be achieved through different structures. For example for the "Movement" from one place to another different living creatures have different structures. Man, cow, bird, snake and fish have different structures foe achieving the purpose of "Movement". There is no 'termini' for the biological functions. In other words what is 'terminus' for a particular biological function is the 'beginning' for several other biological functions. For example the 'corn seeds' which is the terminus for a particular function (for corn crop) may lead to several other biological developments. The corn seeds eaten by birds and goats may lead to different kinds of purposes. In the case of physical and chemical phenomena purpose is invented by human beings. Most of the cosmic and astronomical phenomena are 'accidental' in nature. Man carves out a 'purpose' in a purposeless natural phenomena.

Genetic Explanation

Some of the questions can be answered only if we have the facts relating to the history of a phenomenon. For example "why there is a demand by the Tamils in Sri Lanka for a separate state of Tamil *Eelam*"? The answer can be given by tracing the history of the Sinhalese population who migrated from the Indian states of Orissa and West Bengal after the Kalinga war two millennia years ago. The emperor Ashoka who won the battle is said to have spread the message of Buddhism in Sri Lanka. The migrants from India later on mixed the languages of Pali and Sanskrit with Tamil and a new language of 'Sinhalese' evolved over the centuries. In other words explanation of this kind is based on the analysis of the genesis' of the problem. Any phenomenon whether it is physical, biological or social has its own evolutionary history. Unless we have the facts of the past of a process, the explanation will not be adequate. The present circumstances or factors which may be seemingly the *cause* of a particular phenomenon may not be sufficient in offering an adequate explanation. Therefore genetic explanation plays an important role in the explanation of social phenomenon in particular.

Explanation of Biological Phenomenon

Explanation of physical phenomena and *methodology* adopted to do so is not sufficient to the explanation of Biological phenomena. Mechanistic interpretation of Biological phenomena holds good when 'Biological phenomena' are understood in terms of 'physical' and 'chemical' concepts. In other words 'Reductionism' is followed in understanding Biological processes. But reduction of Biological process into physical and chemical processes will lead to an explanation which is inadequate since Biological phenomena are 'organismic' in nature. The whole is more than the sum of the parts in organismic Biology. The lower order of a biological system 'conditions' the higher order functioning. Each system such as 'digestion', 'blood circulation' and 'brain' are too complex in nature. Each complex system is facilitated by the lower order functions. Each complex function has purpose. All the individual systems perfectly co-ordinate in such a way that the human beings or any other Biological organisms exhibit 'holistic' activities. Mechanical explanations however are not contradictory in the explanation of Biological phenomena. Mechanistic explanations are complemented to Teleological explanations in the complete understanding of Biological phenomena.

Methodological Problems in Social Sciences

Physical and chemical events can be explained by following universal laws which are nomothetic in nature. There are logical and epistemic requirements for scientific explanation. The logical requirements consist in having premises (*Explanans*) which are 'more general' than the *Explanandum*. The premises must contain at least one universal law. The epistemic requirements consist in the premises to be true; the premises must be 'known to be true'. Both logical and epistemic requirements are necessary in Scientific Explanation.

Historical phenomena which are individualistic and unique cannot be explained on the basis of the laws governed by nomothetic sciences. Social sciences are *ideographic* in nature and therefore, the methodology adopted to explain such phenomena is different. Some of the methodological problems that arise when we explain social phenomena are: 1) Controlled Inquiry, 2) Subjective Nature of social subject Matter, 3) Knowledge of social phenomena as a social variable, 4) Value Oriented bias in social inquiry, and 5) Cultural relativity and social laws.[4]

Validity of Scientific Explanation

The scope of scientific explanation is unlimited over nature, including organic and mental phenomena. In the case of purposive behavior a teleological explanation is allowable and mechanistic one is complementary and not rival to it. In the case of *emergents* no explanation is possible; but it may be found with further progress in science. A scientific explanation is not ultimate explanation. For example the scientists are still debating among themselves in finding out the source of 'Corona Virus 19'. So far no satisfactory explanation has been given about the "cause" of such deadly virus which has taken millions of human lives. Yet explanation is a continuous logical as well as psychological process, so that where scientific explanations end, the metaphysical ones begin. Science and philosophy of Science must use higher categories to complete the task of understanding nature.[5]

References

1. A. Appan Ramanujam, *Perspectives of Indian and Western Philosophical Thought*, Sharada Publishing House, New Delhi, 2013, pp. 201-202.

2. Ernest Nagel, *The Structure of Science: Problems in the Logic of Scientific Explanation,* MacMillan Co., London, 1961.
3. A. Appan Ramanujam, *op. cit.,* pp. 202ff.
4. Nagel, *The Structure of Science,* the chapter on "Methodological Problems of Social Sciences", MacMillan Co., London, 1961.
5. *Ibid.*

Chapter X

Science and Humanity

The Social Origin of Science

Science arises out of society to meet certain human needs and it influences and is influenced by society. The social situation sets problems for science and also determines the mode of solutions to some degree while the latter affects the situation itself in its turn. Even religion and politics played roles in creating social situations that led to discoveries in science. There have been continuous and mutual developments between society and history of science. In primitive society magicians claimed that they could cause or check natural phenomena such as rain, storms, sunshine fertility of soil, etc. They didn't know the inductive methods consisting of *observation*, hypothesising, generalisation and verification. But the magician's predictions sometimes failed and the people began to lose faith in the magician's power. Some even thought that some *supernatural agency* must be behind the natural phenomena so that religion and science emerged from the remains of magic. The scientists believed that there was a kind of *uniformity* in the natural phenomena and applied the cause-effect theory. Thus science has its roots in society.[1]

Mutual Interaction of Science and Society

Science has its roots in the society. It springs out of certain fundamental needs of man, the need to live with less frustration in the world where he is placed by his destiny. To fulfill this need he has to study nature and know its habits and manners as it were. Knowing these, he can control nature. Thus the problems of science are set by the practical needs of man. Man's earliest discoveries in the field of agriculture, animal husbandry, metallurgy and engineering were all prompted by his most urgent needs. Later in the history of science we find that the Egyptians discovered geometry for they had to measure lands swept each year by the floods in the river Nile, the sea-faring people living at the coasts discovered navigation. Similarly in course of time steam engine, electric machines, locomotives, railways and aeroplanes were introduced for human needs.

Man's ethical, religious, and psychological tendencies combined with industrial production created situation whereby there was a need felt to govern the people. To transport and sell the goods businessmen emerged. All these social developments led to the formation of a government. Later on different forms of government emerged.[2]

Science and Environment

Environmental science is an interdisciplinary academic field that integrates *physics, biology* and *geography* to the study of the environment, and the solution of environment problems. Environmental science emerged from the fields of natural history and medicine during the Enlightenment. *Environmental studies* incorporates more of the social sciences for understanding human relationships, perceptions and policies towards the environment. *Environmental engineering* focuses on design and technology for improving environmental quality in every aspect.

Environmental scientists seek to understand the earth's physical, chemical biological and geological processes, and to use that knowledge to understand how issues such as *alternative energy* systems, *pollution control* and mitigation, natural resource management, and the effects of global warming and climate change influence and affect the natural systems and processes of earth. Environmental issues include an interaction of physical, chemical and biological processes. Environmental scientists bring a systems approach to the analysis of environmental problems. Key elements of an effective environmental scientists include the ability to relate space and time relationships as well as quantitative analysis.

Alterations in the Environment

Alterations in the environment have been markedly observed especially after the industrial revolution. While exploiting natural resources for his needs, man has changed the natural processes considerably over the past 500 years. As the human population increases these alterations accelerate often to the point of complete depletion and destruction of vegetation cover, water, soil and living resources. Atmospheric pollution caused by automobiles, factories, household fires and nuclear waste further deteriorates the quality of the sunlight rays and atmospheric components. Changes in life style affect the diet, food additives, habitat and additions. Improvement in medical care and therapeutics also increase the number of drugs and antibiotics, increasing our resistance to them and also to the appearance of various bacteria which are resistant to therapy. All these substances may have an effect on the genetic substance and this effect may be transmitted to the next generation.[3]

Scientific and technological progress is one of the principal dangers to the continued existence of Man on this planet. Nuclear energy used for military and industrial purposes, the fast growing chemical industry, extensive use of herbicides and pesticides, genetic engineering and many other such things born of scientific and technological progress may cause irreversible damage to humankind. All these menaces to life can be removed through the very same advances in science and technology.[4] To promote the harmony between Techno-sphere and Biosphere, efforts must be made to regulate consumeristic life style which promotes materialism and global capitalism. Artistic, religious and aesthetic aspects of life must be encouraged. As a student of Nature C.V. Raman, the scientist seeks to resolve her infinite complexities into a few laws of Nature. For him intellectual beauty, which consists of self-consistency, is indeed the highest kind of beauty. Science, in other words, is a fusion of men's aesthetic and intellectual functions devoted to the representation of Nature. It is therefore the highest form of human art. Only men like Buddha, Christ and Mahatma Gandhi, and not scientists could solve human problems by influencing human conduct through an appreciation of spiritual values.

Science and Ethics

Ethical naturalism refers to the science of morality grounding morality in rational empirical consideration of the natural world. It is sometimes framed as using the scientific approach to determine what is right and wrong, in contrast to the widespread belief that science has nothing to say on the subject of human values. In fact a statement of science is considered to be a statement of "fact" whereas an ethical statement is a statement of "value".

Can the quantitative method which is used by science be used in making a statement of morality or can ethics and science be synthesized? Herbert Spencer applies the idea of evolution to morals. He traces the germs of morality to the conduct of animals. According to him life consists in the continuous adjustment of the vital forces to the environment. Conduct is an adjustment of the organism to the environment; that conduct is good which promotes effective adjustment of the organism to the environment and produces pleasure. *That conduct is bad which hinders such adjustment and produces pain. Pleasure is an index of increase of life; pain of decrease of life.* The ultimate end of life is happiness. The proximate end of life is length and breadth of life. Length is duration of life; breadth is volume or complexity of life. Herbert Spencer's Hedonism is called *Evolutionary Hedonism* whereas the Hedonism of Jeremy Bentham and Mill is called Empirical Hedonism. Bentham's Hedonism is also called *quantitative utilitarianism*. He held the view that pleasure can be measured and gave his famous *Hedonistic calculus*. Quantitative technique adopted by scientists was applied by Bentham to the field of morality.

Whenever there is development in biology it has an impact on the morals to be followed. The right or wrong is influenced by the findings of the biologists. Some of the areas in biology which has created moral issues are: abortion, alcoholism, cloning, surrogacy, organ transplantation, terminator seeds in agriculture, etc. However, there are arguments that ethical standards are relative and not absolute. As time passes on the norms which are based on religion society and state have to be revised according to the changed circumstances.

Moral Lesson of Science

Science has certain definite moral consequences on the people cultivating it. If misrepresentative of a case out of one's self-interest or prejudice is a vice, then science is an antidote of it, for it inculcates a respect for facts. The love of rational order is reflected in the social field where too the scientifically minded people like to have proper order and plan instead of chaos and conflict. Men trained in natural science cannot but translate the ideal of rational order into our social behavior, things are not allowed by them to drift. So that ethics and sociology are approached in a scientific manner. The present moral problems may be cured to a large extent if we substitute a scientific method of enquiry in these fields for prejudice and dogmatism. Science has no extra rational interest to serve, be it personal or national, and it does not know any authority, whether scriptural or traditional. Science owes no loyalty to anything but facts, reason and harmonious order. Whatever policy will bring about the greatest possible coherence in the society will be recommended by it. Again science favors the democratic principle of equality of all men, for men are for science and technology subjects who know and do and as such are valued irrespective of their nationality, caste and creed, complexion or habits of eating and dressing.[5] Science is a co-operative enterprise on a global scale. In short by following scientific method in ethics and sociology most of the ills of the society can be cured. Such method will overcome the prejudices based on race, religion geography, politics, culture and language.

Science and Religion

Science and religion offer explanations for why life and the universe exist. Science relies on testable empirical evidence and observation. Religion relies on subjective belief in a creator. Religion is based on authority and science is based on observation and reason. Modern science has discovered the precise demonstrable laws of nature, a blind power in the inorganic and the organic world, the vastness of the universe in time and in extension of which all things are parts, and a certain periodicity in cosmic order. Naturally these discoveries cannot but influence one's overall attitude to the world and, so, one's essential faith governing his behavior. This new faith may be called 'naturalistic religion' or 'the religion of science'.

Copernicus, Kepler, Galileo and Newton revealed that the world moved according to the laws of mathematics. They believed in some cosmic order which is not teleological, but mechanical. It is neither man created nor God created. As such it is indifferent to our human interests. Whether individual or collective, and our task lies in only knowing this vast impartial order.[6]

The scientist's belief in a cosmic order which regulates the vast universe mechanically had already been revealed by the Chinese *Tao,* the Greek *Nemesis* or Fate and the Indian *Rta.* Resignation to the impersonal and blind order may be cheerful and dignified as may be found in *Confucius and Spinoza.*

True religion ensures the dignity of man though it teaches him humility. A spiritual religion is needed to complement a naturalistic one and to correct some of his faults. A supernatural to religion is needed to complement a naturalistic one and to correct some of his faults. A supernatural force is like God who has free will and is essential for the strength and happiness of man. The unending vastness of the universe and man's feeling of insignificance makes him dejected. A sense of teleology and worthiness of his existence is needed for man. Though science can offer explanations for the working of the universe through his rational analysis there are many questions which it cannot answer. Whether soul exists or not? What is the destiny of soul? Why there is good or evil? Therefore religion teaches science that it has limitations. Spiritualistic religion can show that God is merciful and benevolent person who wields the power of love rather than of hatred.

Integration of Science and Religion

Whitehead's process philosophy is a promising way to integrate science and religion. Science and religion are closely interconnected in the scientific study of religion. Natural historians attempted to provide naturalistic explanations for human behavior and culture, for domains such as religion, emotions and morality. For example Bernard de Fontenelle offered a causal account of belief in the Supernatural. People often assert Supernatural explanations when they lack an understanding of the natural causes underlying extraordinary events. Auguste Comte believed that myths would gradually give way to scientific accounts. Hume's *Natural History of Religion* is the best known philosophical example of a natural historical explanation of religious beliefs. It traces the origin of polytheism to ignorance about natural causes combined with fear and apprehension about the environment. By deifying aspects of the environment, early humans tried to persuade or bribe the gods, thereby gaining a sense of control. Similar attempts by the early Vedic Aryans resulted in the worship of the natural forces: *Agni, Vayu* and *Varuna*. Emile Durkheim considered religious beliefs as a social glue that helped to keep society together. Sigmund Freud saw religious belief as an illusion, a child like yearning for a father figure. William James was interested in the psychological roots and the phenomenology of religious experiences. A recent development in the scientific study of religion is the cognitive science of religion. This is a multidisciplinary field, with authors from among others, developmental psychology, anthropology, philosophy and cognitive psychology. It differs from the other scientific approaches to religion by its presupposition that religion is not a purely cultural phenomenon but the result of ordinary, early developed and universal human cognitive processes. Another hypothesis regards religion as a biological or cultural adaptive response that helps humans solve co-operative problems

Science and Art

Traditionally, art and science have been treated as two separate disciplines, but when they are studied together it is clear to see the impact one has on the other. A great deal of creativity is required to make scientific breakthrough, and art is just as often an expression of (or a product of) scientific knowledge. Consider the science behind mixing paint in the correct proportions. Visual art has been used to document the natural world for thousands of years, from cave drawings of animals that help today's researchers figure out yesterday's fauna, to paintings of centuries-old experiments that show us how they were conducted. One of the most famous examples of the interconnection between art and science is the work of Renaissance master *Leonardo da Vinci.*

While his *Mona Lisa* is probably the most famous portrait ever painted, da Vinci's scientific drawings are smaller in scale and intricately detailed and annotated. Da Vinci conducted his own experiments and studies. Wordsworth and Shelley treated analytical reason ruling science as inferior to, and, in fact, a handmaid, of synthetic imagination that operates in poetry. Imagination, or poetry which is the expression of it, is the 'breadth and finer spirit of all knowledge, while science only murders to dissect'. But though art is not concerned about facts and figures, it is not indifferent to truth of human life and emotions. Science is not a work of bare analysis without involving any imaginative integration. The fact is that both the artist and the scientist seek to comprehend a large number of phenomena by means of a short expression which becomes symbolical of the class of phenomena it represents. "Thus the law of gravity or thermal expansion in science and a certain character in drama or a telling phrase in poetry or a drawing in art serves the same end. Both analysis are involved in this process of comprehension, for we have to distinguish and select objects from the rich confusion of them presented before us in order to arrange then into a class by virtue of their common trait, contiguity is space and time, or causal relation, and we have to hold them together under a common concept or law, express either in words or mathematical symbols".[7] There is no essential difference between art and science either in matter or in form. The matter is all human experience and the form is organization of it through analysis and synthesis and representation in spoken words or symbols. The difference lies in the prevailing interest operating in each; science is interested in the experiences which are more amenable to measurement and exact mathematical formulations while art is interested in those which have an appeal to human emotions and feelings. Art seeks to represent, not particular facts, but human feeling and values. In the case of science, one must have sharp and trained senses and a mathematical intellect, while in the case of art he must have emotional and imaginative nature and a cultivated taste besides an acquaintance with the medium of art he wishes to appreciate. Science is interested in one kind of experience that tell one version of a mystery tale while there are other kinds of experience and other versions of the tale. The artists are interested in these other kinds and a normal human being must be interested in all the kinds. Devotion to one of the diverse approaches to the secret of reality to the exclusion of others would be nothing but an act of self-denial; it would be like employing only one of the several senses and suspending the rest for our acquaintance of the perceptual world.[8]

References

1. P.K. Sengupta, *Pravas Jivan Chaudhury on Multi-Aspects of Philosophy*, Indian Council of Philosophical Research, New Delhi, p. 217.

2. *Ibid.*, pp. 218-219.

3. Geeta Talukder, "Environmental Hazards and the Future of Human Development", In *Holistic Human Concern for World Welfare*, The Theosophical Society, Chennai, p. 55.

4. Nikita Moiseyev, "Technosphere and Biosphere a Search for Harmony", In *Holistic Human Concern for World Welfare*, The Theosophical Society, Chennai, p. 44.

5. P.K. Sengupta, *op. cit.*, pp. 224-225.

6. *Ibid.*, p. 227.

7. *Ibid.*, p. 233.

8. *Ibid.*, p. 235.

Bibliography

Alexander, S., *Space, Time and Deity*, MacMillan, London.

Ayer, A.J. (1946) *Language, Truth and Logic*, Victor Gollancz, London.

Bandiste, D.D. (2005) *Manual of Philosophy of Science*, B.R. Publishing Corporation, Delhi.

Bencerraf, Paul and Hilary Putnam (eds.) (2004) *Philosophy of Mathematics*, Cambridge University Press.

Bergson, H. (1911) *Creative Evolution*, trans. by Arthur Mitchell, Macmillan & Co., London.

Bhaskar, Roy (1979) *The Possibilities of Naturalism: A Philosophical Critique of the Contemporary Human Sciences*, The Harvester Press, Brighton, Sussex.

Bohm, D. (1957) *Causality and Chance in Modern Physics*, Routledge and Kegan Paul, London.

Bostock, David (2009) *Philosophy of Mathematics - An Introduction*, Wiley-Blackwell, Oxford.

Caws, Peter (1965) *The Philosophy of Science: A Systematic Account*, D. Van Nostrand Co., New Jersey, first edition.

Darwin, Charles (1903) *Origin of Species*, Watts & Co., London.

Durban, Paul R. (1968) *Philosophy of Science*, McGraw Hill Book Company, New York.

Eddington, A.S. (1928) *The Nature of the Physical World*, Cambridge Scholars Publishing.

Einstein, A. (1922) *Sidelights of Relativity*, Methuen & Co, London.

Frank, P. (2004) *Philosophy of Science: The Link Between Science and Philosophy*, Dover Publications.

Hart, W.D. (ed.) (1996) *The Philosophy of Mathematics*, Oxford University Press, Oxford.

Hear, Anthony O' (1989) *An Introduction to Philosophy of Science*, Clarendon Press.

Heisenberg, W. and Arthur H. Compton (1930) *The Physical Principles of Quantum Theory*, University of Chicago Press, Chicago.

Hempel, Carl G. and Paul Oppenheim (1948) 'Studies in the Logic of Explanation', *Philosophy of Science*, 15(2).

Irvine, Andrew D. (2009) *Philosophy of Mathematics (Handbook of the Philosophy of Science)*, North Holland Vancouver, Canada.

Jardine, N. (1988) *The Birth of History and Philosophy of Science: Kepler's 'A Defence of Tycho Against Ursus' with Essays on Its Provenance and Significance*, Cambridge University Press, New York.

Kant, I. (1950) *Critique of Pure Reason*, trans. by Norman Kemp Smith, Macmillan & Co., London.

Körner, Stephan (2009) *The Philosophy of Mathematics: An Introductory Essay*, Dover Publication Inc., USA.

Kuhn, Thomas (1962) *The Structure of Scientific Revolution* Chicago University Press, Chicago.

Nagel, E. (1961) *The Structure of Science: Problems in the Logic of*

Scientific Explanation, Harcourt-Brace & World Inc., New York.

Nandivarman, Pudhuvai (n.d) *The Land of the Tamils and their Unique Culture*, Arjuna Padhippagam, Chennai.

Paseau, Alexander (ed.) (2017) *Philosophy of Mathematics*, Routledge, London.

Pietro Redondi and P.V. Pillai (1989) *The History of Sciences: The French Debate*, Orient Longman, New Delhi.

Planck, M. (1933) *Where is Science Going?*, Allen & Unwin, London.

Popper, Karl R. (1959) *The Logic of Scientific Discovery*, Hutchinson & Co., London.

Popper, Karl R. (1962) *Conjectures and Refutations: The Growth of Scientific Knowledge*, Routledge, London.

Popper, Karl (1945) *The Open Society and its Enemies*, 2 Vols., Routledge, London.

Popper, Karl (1957) *The Poverty of Historicism*, Routledge, London.

Ram Harre (1972) *The Philosophy of Science*, Oxford University Press, London.

Russell, B. (1919) *Introduction to Mathematical Philosophy*, George Allen & Unwin Ltd., London.

Russell, B. (1914) *Our Knowledge of the External World: As a Field for Scientific Method in Philosophy*, Routledge, New York.

Sengupta, P.K. (2003) *Pravas Jivan Chaudhury on Multi-Aspects of Philosophy*, Indian Council of Philosophical Research, New Delhi.

Sepkoski, David (2007) *Nominalism and Constructivism in Seventeenth Century Mathematical Philosophy*, Routledge, New York.

Shapiro, Stewart (1997) *Philosophy of Mathematics (Structure and Ontology)*, Oxford University Press, New York.

Shaw, James Byrians (2008) *Lectures on The Philosophy of Mathematics*, Cosmo Publications, New Delhi.

Swami Abhedananda (2011) *A Study of Heliocentric Science*, Ramakrishna Vedanta Math, Kolkata.

Tieszen, Richard (2005) *Phenomenology, Logic and The Philosophy of Mathematics*, Cambridge University Press.

Index